KNOWING THE TRUTH ABOUT
HEAVEN AND HELL

Knowing the Truth about Heaven and Hell

Our Choices and Where They Lead Us

Harry Blamires

SERVANT BOOKS
Ann Arbor, Michigan

Published by Servant Books
P.O. Box 8617
Ann Arbor, Michigan 48107

Scripture texts in this work are taken from *The King James Version* of the Bible, unless otherwise indicated.

Cover design by Steve Eames
Cover illustration by Douglas A. Bowles

88 89 90 91 92 10 9 8 7 6 5 4 3 2 1

Printed in the United States of America
ISBN 0-89283-370-X

Library of Congress Cataloging-in-Publication Data

Blamires, Harry.
  Knowing the truth about heaven and hell.

  (Knowing the truth)
  1. Heaven. 2. Hell. 3. Eschatology. I. Title. II. Series.
BT846.2.B53   1988   236'.24   88-6568
ISBN 0-89283-370-X

Contents

Publisher's Preface

Servant Books is a publishing outreach of The Sword of the Spirit, an international Christian community whose members represent virtually every stream of church tradition: Protestant, Catholic, and Orthodox. While respecting the differences that divide them, members of The Sword of the Spirit are able to live and serve the Lord together in a united way by focusing on the foundational truths that all faithful Christians hold in common.

Books in the *Knowing the Truth* series aim to express these core realities of the faith in a way that helps all Christians recognize and appreciate the treasures of our shared heritage.

John C. Blattner
Servant Publications

General Editors' Preface

Books in this series have a threefold purpose: to make disciples of Jesus Christ, to lead Christians on to maturity, and to advance the cause of unity within Christ's church. The goal is to convince, edify, and unify by responding to the challenges of unbelief, the cry of spiritual hunger, and the schismatic attitudes of mind and heart that press upon us so hard at the present time.

Our situation is one in which dissent and departure from the essentials of the Christian faith, as revealed in the Bible and set forth in the Creeds, grow steadily worse. The crisis of pluralism escalates, and this bewilders new inquirers, unsettles old saints, disrupts the internal fellowship of churches, and undermines the work of shepherding the flock and evangelizing the world. It is this situation that has called the series into being.

The editors and authors are united in their conviction of the truth and wisdom of the "old paths" of what C.S. Lewis called "mere Christianity"—the ancient orthodox faith on which all Christians fed for the first eighteen centuries. This common belief is no vague, weak "lowest common denominator," but a solid, wide-ranging spread of belief and practice that has been at the heart of every mainstream Christian body from apostolic times.

In many centers of so-called Christian teaching today, clear and definite truth—revealed truth or dogma, to use the time-honored terms—is no longer thought to be available. What formerly went under these names is dismissed as culturally determined fancy, and fresh fancies that are only too obviously spin-offs from modern secular thought are set in their place.

This is a tide that we hope our series will help to turn.

The writers' liberty to express their views has not been restricted in any way. Each addresses a readership that includes Roman Catholics, Protestants, and Orthodox Christians, presenting basic truths on which these heritages have at their best been one and commending them as wisdom urgently needed at this time. Each believes and strives to observe the sound old maxim: "In essentials, unity; in nonessentials, liberty; in all things, charity."

These expositions of Bible-based, Christ-centered, Spirit-taught, church-oriented, life-changing Christianity now go out with the prayer that in showing forth the common core of Christianity, they will present clear and cogent testimony to our bemused world, and effectively stabilize and build up the people of God.

J.I. Packer
Peter Kreeft

Introduction

THE PURPOSE OF THIS BOOK is to explore the traditional Christian teaching about heaven and hell. The book is not therefore an exercise in original thinking. I have never thought that it was the business of the Christian teacher to indulge in private speculation. The teacher's task is to explore the traditional faith of Christendom, which is rooted in the Scriptures, and to do one's best to elucidate it for the benefit of others. Dealing with the life hereafter, however, presents special problems. It is not possible to speak with the same certainty of life in eternity as it is to speak of doctrines directly earthed in human history.

Indeed, I must make it clear that I have shared all the questionings that the reader has experienced when trying to grapple with Christian teaching about the afterlife. Like my reader, I first want to know exactly what mainstream Christian teaching about heaven and hell amounts to. And then I want to know how the traditional teaching about eternal punishment can be squared with the message of God's love and mercy. We must not pretend that this is a simple and straightforward matter. If it were, I could have written this book differently. I could have made it an exercise in direct instruction: What you need to know about heaven and hell!

I have chosen a different method of approach. I live in the same environment as the reader, an environment hostile to the supernatural dimensions of the Christian faith. All around us, even within the church, are attitudes of mind that tend to tear Christian teaching away from its moorings in supernatural reality. I want to move at the reader's side from the world where doctrines of heaven and hell are regarded as fanciful or totally unacceptable, into that sphere of belief where Christ's words about the hereafter are taken as seriously as his words about loving and forgiving. I want to be at the reader's elbow, sharing his or her questionings, and using the map of revelation and the torch of reason to guide us together to the truth.

That is why this book tackles first a question crucial to full understanding of Christian teaching: Is there a place for punishment in the divine government of mankind? When that problem has been dealt with, a second question is tackled. Christ offered salvation to men and women who respond to his call. Then what is the alternative to salvation for those who reject his offer? From these two questions the book turns to examine the nature of evil and what it must mean to be condemned to hell.

It should go without saying that the writer's (and the reader's) progress through such considerations is a journey where landmarks are sometimes hazy and where signposts may be hard to decipher. What else can we expect when we have the presumption to set out in exploration of mysteries so profound as those of the afterlife?

In particular, when this book turns in chapter four to consider Christian teaching about the Second Coming, the judgment, and more especially the possible interim state known as purgatory, any claim to speak decisively on all points for Christendom as a whole must be dropped. All the writer can do is to record objectively various views which Christians hold. Of course, every effort must be made to keep personal bias out of the picture.

The task becomes more congenial when we turn in the last chapters to the subject of heaven. Biblical teaching about heaven may be highly charged with imagery, but that imagery has an unmistakable message for us. Choosing between heaven and hell is the weightiest human concern on earth, and it is with us every day of our lives. Though there may be areas of confusion in interpreting the biblical view of the afterlife, we can be grateful for the decisiveness of Scripture on this ultimate issue. The stark contrast between the attainment and the loss of eternal blessedness is always vigorously pressed home.

I have used the King James Bible throughout this study for three reasons. The first reason is that it is the only version of the Bible with which I personally am sufficiently acquainted for its phrases to run naturally in my mind. The second reason is that, from time to time in this book, I make reference to the thought and work of writers for whom the King James Bible was likewise the text that threaded itself through their thought and writings. The third reason is that, as a specialist in English literature, I feel a special obligation towards keeping alive a text whose phrases have permeated the intellectual lives of English writers of the last few centuries, echoing and re-echoing in their work.

ONE

Is Punishment Necessary?

What Justice Demands

When I was a very young child in the 1920s the shadows of the recent Great War hung over British life. "The War" seemed to be what adults blamed for most of the great miseries that many people plainly had to endure. Throughout the school days of my generation we were surrounded by contemporaries who had lost their fathers and were being brought up by widowed mothers, often living with grandmothers or spinster aunts. Spinster aunts were certainly thick on the ground. There was a husbandless generation as well as a fatherless one. It was largely due to the slaughter on the Western front and at Gallipoli. Many of the children I knew lived on a local housing estate which had been hurriedly built to fulfill Prime Minister Lloyd George's promise to provide "homes for heroes." When I got inside one of these little semi-detached dwellings, I found that having a hero for a father might be even more dismal and tragic than having no father at all. Here was a friend, Albert, whose father sat propped up—frail, pale, shapeless, and gasping for breath. Gassed and wounded at the front, he now occupied himself with an iron contraption sprouting wheels, levers, and pedals, which I was told was a sock-making machine.

What happened to the socks? Perhaps they found their way into those battered suitcases which ex-servicemen used to carry around from house to house. They would knock on the door and, when it was opened, lay the case down on the step to prevent the door from being closed in their faces. They lifted the lid to display for sale a collection of dusters, scrub brushes, dishcloths, boot laces, reels of cotton, shoe polish, buttons, elastic, and other miscellany. My mother always bought something, explaining to her children that the man's dismal need to earn a living in this way was due to the War.

These hawkers did at least, generally speaking, have the usual number of arms and legs, eyes and ears. Their less fortunate fellows tended to ply their trade standing in the gutter in busy shopping streets in the city center. A man would hang a piece of cardboard around his neck, reading "Wounded on the Somme," and stand there holding a tray laden with boxes of matches or, at Christmas, with balloons and paper streamers. Sympathetic shoppers would throw coins on to the tray, but it was more or less understood that you did not bother to pick up the wares you had supposedly purchased. If you did, you were likely to find a secondhand matchbox containing only about a third of the full number of matches.

It was said by adults that not all such claimants to public sympathy were genuine ex-servicemen. But where a leg, or an arm, or an eye, or a section of face was missing, the claim to sympathy could scarcely be disputed. Indeed, in the case of the most brutally disfigured heroes it was not even necessary to pretend to be trading wares. A notice reading "Wounded on the Somme," strung around the neck below an eyeless face and above hands holding a begging bowl, would touch the hearts of passers-by.

"What's the Somme, Mummy?" a curious child would ask in passing. "It was the War. There was a big battle. The Germans must have shot him in the face," the mother would reply.

There were no television pictures to fill out the details, but most homes had their collections of illustrated magazines recording recent history. Besides, the cinemas were always advertising war films with titles like *Ypres* and *The Guns of Loos*, their marquees depicting soldiers and tanks in the thick of battle.

The horrors of the carnage were not difficult for a child to grasp. If parents kept us away from the violent war films, we got an idea of the battlefield when Charlie Chaplin donned a uniform and they tried vainly to turn him into a soldier. As for the cause of it all, the wicked Germans were responsible. And savage as the years of slaughter had been, the one great consolation was that the Germans had been thoroughly beaten. Justice had been done.

But had justice really been done? The child was not so sure. For from time to time in the 1920s, when there was no sensational current event to report and no newsy photograph to print, British newspapers would fall back on a picture of the ex-Kaiser, "walking yesterday in the woods of his estate at Doorn." There, large as life, was the arch villain who had personally willed World War I, walking with two legs and two arms, not to mention eyes and ears. Even a child knew that not having a palace with a throne to sit on—not having a kingdom to rule or a court to enjoy—must be quite a deprivation. But it was a sight better to be walking in the woods at Doorn than to be selling matches in a city gutter.

If wickedness ought to be paid for, there was little evidence here that justice was being done. If anybody was paying the price of wickedness, it was certainly not the ex-Kaiser. Would it not have been *better, right,* and *just,* for the ex-Kaiser to be in Albert's father's place, white-faced, emaciated, and crumpled, trembling and gasping over his sock-making machine?

A young child protests indignantly against the injustice of a world which leaves the perpetrator of mass slaughter declining comfortably into old age with three good meals a day and no need to exert himself other than to keep his body fit. Meanwhile, millions of victims of his selfish policies have either had their lives cut short or their physical or mental well-being shattered.

A more mature person would question whether the ex-

Kaiser did not suffer a good deal from remorse and self-blame, even if it was chiefly over the fact that he did not manage to win the war he started. But such speculation can scarcely cancel out the appalling contrast between the price of his actions paid by Albert's father and millions like him and the price paid by the perpetrator himself.

A reader may well reflect at this point that there is scarcely need to go back to the ex-Kaiser and World War I to point out the distinction between the fate of the perpetrators and the fate of their victims. However wicked the ex-Kaiser may have been, clearly his record pales beside that of Adolf Hitler and his henchmen. The case of the Kaiser was cited because a child—innocent in the ways of the world—could not but insist that justice required the Kaiser to get a taste of Albert's father's experience.

So general was just such a demand for justice after World War II that the initiators of its horrors were arraigned as war criminals and charged in open court. But was justice done? Hitler shot himself. Goering, Himmler, and Goebbels swallowed cyanide. Did their fate in any way match up to the miseries of those who had been stripped, tortured, marched into gas chambers, and then buried in mass graves? Did the villains get a taste of their own medicine?

We cannot feel convinced that they did. Are we wicked for feeling that they certainly *ought* to have paid a price? After all, this feeling does not necessarily have anything to do with the impulse to get revenge for injury that we have suffered personally. We need not have been directly harmed by the war. We need not have had relatives among those tortured and killed by the Gestapo to feel convinced that a price should be paid.

Is it vengeful to demand punishment of those who have harmed others and not ourselves? Is it not healthy to feel outraged when brutal savageries, such as the Holocaust, fail to bring punishment to the perpetrators? If such offenses were never to be punished, would they not cry out that there must be something untrustworthy, something indeed perverse, at the heart of creation? And by something perverse I mean something that is irreconcilable with justice, truth, and even love.

Certain fallacies in current thinking have clouded our understanding of punishment. We tend to think that if a man has done injury to another, no good can be served by doing a legalized injury to the man himself. "Two wrongs don't make a right," it is said of retributory punishment. Indeed it is argued that there is no place for retribution in our prison system.

But that is nonsense. To pretend that prison sentences can be justified only as a means of rehabilitation and as a way of deterring crime is absurd. The only possible justification for depriving a sane man of his liberty is that he has committed an offense which must be punished. Retribution is the only moral justification for imprisonment. Deterrence, as a justification for imprisonment, is actually immoral.

To imprison a man because he has assaulted a policeman is fair enough. But to imprison a man because someone else in the future might or might not assault a policeman is both unjust and immoral. You can justly deprive people of their liberty only for offenses they have actually committed and not for offenses which other people might be tempted to commit. The fact that few of our contemporaries are capable of straight thinking on this matter of earthly punishment for civil offenses suggests that they are unlikely to think straight on the matter of divine or human punishment for moral offenses.

Many honest Christians have had their natural good sense corrupted by a false conception of what Christian charity and compassion require. We are told to forgive those who have injured us. We are not told to forgive the hoodlums who brutally beat the widow next door in order to steal her savings. We are not in a position to forgive them. Only she and God can forgive them. Certainly we are to hope that the time will come when everyone can forgive them. But first things first.

If we have any love at all for our battered, bleeding neighbor, we shall insist that those who willfully struck her down should get to know and to feel exactly what they have done. That is, or ought to be, the nature of punishment. The suffering is a consequence or a by-product of learning what you have done, in short of facing the truth. That is why we said that justice, love, and truth demand punishment.

It does not mean that justice, love, and truth recommend hitting a man where it hurts, locking him up, or otherwise tormenting him, as an end in itself. It means that justice, love, and truth demand that self-deception should be unmasked. The true character of the man and what he has done must be made plain to every wrongdoer.

The unmasking of self-deception is always an act of love. You would surely think it unfriendly if people conspired to keep the truth about your own behavior from you. There can be no rehabilitation without self-knowledge, and rehabilitation is certainly what love demands. Love wants what truth wants, and truth wants what justice wants.

What does facing the truth amount to in the case of the racketeering godfather whose worldwide empire of heroin smuggling has poisoned the lives of thousands of men and women and made wretched the lives of thousands more of their loved ones? His case is clearly comparable to that of the Kaiser or Hitler. In any situation in which wrongs were to be righted and the evils that we do brought home to us, surely such villains would have to face thousands or millions of fellow human beings who would say simply: "Your lust for cash or your lust for power cost me my life or my happiness."

All the millions of wounded, all the slaughtered, all the damaged in mind and body, and all those kin and friends who shared their sufferings would have to confront the persecutors and cry out together in their grief and anger, "This is what you did to us." They would have to spell it out case by case, wound by wound, misery by misery, hammering the facts into the hearts and minds of the villains. Until the time when that happens, there is unfinished business indeed so far as justice and love are concerned. And that unfinished business is incalculable in scope.

Suppose we try to picture what justice requires for the closing of Adolf Hitler's human account. We find ourselves with a scene of overwhelming magnitude. All those millions of wronged souls clamor to get in a word. Every claim is a cry of protest at the willful cruelty and butchery endured. Yet I have just read a newspaper article which questions whether modern Christians still believe in hell, because the idea of eternal punishment is assumed to be irreconcilable with everything that is "humane, civilized, decent, and liberal."

We need not linger yet over the word *eternal*. Any punishment after death must be *eternal* in the sense that it will be outside time. But where is this modern Christian who is so *humane, civilized, decent,* and *liberal* that he thinks the human account should be fully closed at death, the human scenario equipped with a happy ending, for those who actively and willfully wrought upon their fellows the horrors of the Holocaust?

As I understand the words *humane, civilized, decent,* and even *liberal,* I should have declared that every impulse of humanity, civilized decency, and true liberality would demand for them a face-to-face reckoning with what they did, a confrontation with the truth, and thus an experience of punishment. Indeed, to try to shelter such horrific wrongdoing from justice and its penalties is to be on the side of barbarism against civilization.

Closing Life's Account

It is not within the scope of earthly life to bring the truth about himself and his deeds home to every man. A Hitler, a Himmler, an Eichmann, or a Stalin can only die once. At their death there may be a sense of satisfaction that the world has been cleansed of their presence. But there is no conviction that they have faced a true reckoning of what they have done to others. Justice and truth demand that they should. Love too demands that they should, love for their victims and love for themselves. It is necessary to consider these two forms of *love* together. Our love for their victims is based on natural compassion for all who suffer innocently. Our love for them involves the cool, rational recognition that self-deception must be cleared away and truth made evident to them.

It is not improper to define that attitude to the wicked as an expression of love. The impulse which sends you out to visit a charming, unselfish old lady who bears her afflictions with good humor is not all that different from the impulse which bids you call on the bitter, cantankerous old lady who is forever grumbling about her ailments. The one is an attractive person you naturally like. The other is an unattractive person you try not to dislike. What sends you out to visit both is Christian love.

Now there are degrees of repulsion as there are degrees of attraction. The ill-tempered old lady ought not to be classified in her unattractiveness alongside either a Hitler or a hoodlum who beats up an old-age pensioner in search of her cash. But the principle is firm that Christian love must operate towards those who are most repulsive to us.

Our argument has concentrated so far largely on the infamous tyrants whose evil deeds have stained the public history of our century. Their cases only magnify a problem which affects us all in our daily life. It would be natural for the reader to feel that so long as we focus our thoughts on the fate of evil public figures we are evading concerns that strike closer to home. What is going to happen *eternally* to that difficult neighbor who never has a kind word for anyone? Or what will happen to the arrogant boss who treats his or her subordinates like dirt? Certainly it is a challenge to know what Christian love requires of us when we deal with people who—at a far less spectacular and damaging level than an evil tyrant—indulge in a degree of self-deception which makes them difficult to like and sometimes impossible to advise.

We have all met such people. If they are in positions of

authority, they exercise that authority in complete ignorance of the effect they have on others. They cannot endure opposition. They cannot bear to have their own opinions questioned. They suspect anyone who does not flatter and applaud them. They obsessively try to keep their hands on absolutely everything that happens within their sphere of influence. You can watch such people being lured ever deeper and deeper into a mental world from which all give-and-take is excluded by their psychological need to be top dog, to be forever right.

Their vanity wraps them around in a cocoon of self-centeredness which cushions them from reality. If they are professing Christians, they manage to turn even their Christianity into a means of insulating themselves from criticism or opposition. They make much of Christian charity and community spirit. By such talk they stifle open disagreement with any of their personal fads or prejudices. In the extreme case a Mr. Whiterthan White, without knowing what he is doing, can rationalize Christian love into the duty of others to keep him happy by never resisting his slightest whim.

Christian love is robust and unsentimental. It would surely like to see Mr. White dragged from the emotional morass of his personal vanity. We are told that we must love our neighbors as ourselves, and none of us would wish to be left undisturbed in Mr. White's moral condition. None of us would want to be so cut off from reality as he is. Love, in short, would require him to be checked in his course, to be given a rude awakening to what he is. He must learn what kind of motives have swayed him. He must come to see what kind of a figure he cuts in other people's eyes.

The effects of such an awakening are inevitably punishing. But truth and love demand the awakening. Yet it very often does not happen in this life at all. Again, as love sees it, this life on earth presents us with an unfinished scenario. It is so in the case of the great villains of history. It is so in the case of many ordinary mortals whom we would not classify as wicked.

Suppose the awakening to truth *does* happen in this life, and suppose it leads to penitence, does that necessarily close the human account for good and all? There are cases where criminals have repented of the gravest crimes, where conversion during imprisonment has brought people to a new life of faith and good works. In such cases can we declare the human account closed? A sentence of imprisonment has been served. An earthly penalty has been paid. God's forgiveness has been asked. Does not this round off the human story with a happy ending? Does it not render any reckoning hereafter redundant?

Alas, it must be rare indeed for the business of life to be fully finished in the eyes of justice, in the eyes of truth, and in the eyes of love. The denouement of an earthly comedy requires the unmasking of the villain before the very eyes of the hero he tried to trick out of his happiness. The completion of the scenario of our lives would seem to require the unmasking of our damaging acts, great or small, before the eyes of those we have damaged. Yet, you will say, in Christianity the name of the game is forgiveness. Indeed, but forgiveness can be given and received only when the offender and offended fully recognize the offense for what it is; and this is bound to be painful for the offender.

One of the most shocking crimes of our age was committed in the United Kingdom in 1965. Ian Brady and Myra Hindley were charged with the murder of three children. The murders had been preceded by brutal sexual molestation. The prosecution produced tape recordings of the voices of the murderers with the screams and protests of a ten-year-old girl whom they killed. The children's corpses were driven up on to the bleak Pennine moors and buried by night.

And now, twenty years later, the police are seeking in the same area for the buried bodies of two other child victims of the convicted couple. There is no need to pile up adjectives to express a proper human response to these crimes. The facts speak for themselves. Ian Brady and Myra Hindley are serving life sentences and it is urged by many that neither should ever be released.

Brady, it seems, was the mastermind behind the operation. Nothing is publicly known of his attitude now. He is under psychiatric treatment. Myra Hindley was in love with him and could certainly be regarded as uniquely unfortunate in meeting and falling in love with such a man. One may question whether, without that circumstance, she would ever have found herself convicted of a crime. Moreover, she was reared a Christian. The effects of this have surfaced since her imprisonment. It is known that she has experienced deep remorse and contrition Fully acknowledging her sinfulness, she has sought that forgiveness which is promised without reserve to all who are truly penitent.

For purposes of our argument, the case of Ian Brady is not problematic. He has not made any public acknowledgment of the wrong he has done. In that respect he is another of whom it may be said that, morally speaking, the account is unfinished. But Myra Hindley has made gestures that indicate her deep sorrow for the miseries she has caused. There is no reason to doubt her genuine contrition. She has apparently faced the truth about herself before God and has suffered in doing so. There has been talk of contact between her and the mother of one of her victims.

Even so, it seems doubtful whether any such development could fully close the moral account here below. This is not to question that God may have forgiven Myra Hindley for her involvement in murder, just as we hope we are forgiven for entertaining those malicious thoughts which our Lord assures us are the moral equivalents of her crimes. But there seems to be something here which is not fully settled at the human level by divine forgiveness. Myra Hindley may one day actually meet the mother of one of her victims and may beg her forgiveness. And the mother may respond in all mercy and charity, saying "I forgive you for depriving me of my child." But is that enough to close the account? What the mother cannot possibly add is,

"I forgive you for depriving my child of her life." Only the child herself could grant forgiveness for that. There is no earthly possibility of fully closing the account in this respect.

This fact puts murder as a sin in a peculiarly painful category. When the sin is fully repented of, the offender cannot beg pardon of the offended. This is not said in order to make Myra Hindley's lot seem the more unbearable. On the contrary. After all, the apostle Paul himself was an accessory to murder as a witness to the stoning of the martyr Stephen. And he had no opportunity to beg pardon of the martyr.

Is it always impossible, in terms of justice and love, fully to close the account of a human career on earth? There would seem to be demands which both justice and love will make that cannot be answered here below. Each of us, reader and writer, has his or her own recollections of accounts that in human terms cannot be fully squared, even though the sins involved may have been confessed and divinely forgiven.

In youth, we borrowed something which, through a mixture of forgetfulness and apathy, we failed ever to return to a lender who could ill afford to do without it. But the person is now long dead. At school, we played a part in baiting a shy classmate or a nervous teacher, making their life a misery. We joined with others in mocking the foibles of some eccentric older person who gradually sensed that he or she was being made a laughingstock, so that bitterness was added to loneliness.

We think of this treatment now with remorse and compassion, but the victims are dead or out of our reach. There were people we belittled, people we misjudged, people we misrepresented, people we cold-shouldered, and they are all gone. There were even offenses unknowingly committed which we would like to see opened up like washed linen on the clothesline and aired by the wind. How were we to know that someone's cool treatment of us, which provoked a withering response, was after all the product of mental instability, or of unjust pressure exerted by another?

The people we offended, lightly or gravely, long ago and not so long ago, are all now dead. In that respect they are like Myra Hindley's victims. They leave us with an account which in human terms cannot be fully closed on earth.

What Love Demands

The reader will note that I have made no appeals to Scripture in the argument so far. That is intentional. For I have noticed a general tendency when Christians write about hell, which I am anxious to avoid. It is difficult to define this tendency exactly. Let me call it the "good-heavens-what-have-we-here?" approach I call it that because writers tend to start their consideration of the doctrine of hell by quite properly insisting that God is the God of love. They then turn up texts in the Bible which refer to everlasting torment with what I call the "good-heavens-what-have-we-here?" attitude.

Christianity is a religion of love, but here is a text which speaks of condemnation of the wicked to everlasting fire. What can we make of that? How can we reconcile the idea of hell with the notion of a loving God?

I have not pursued this line of argument for reasons which I hope are gradually becoming apparent to the reader as my own line of reasoning becomes clear. From all serious observation of the human scene with the eye of love, it becomes evident, before turning to Scripture, that love demands a reckoning hereafter. And that reckoning must involve punishment. That punishment must be eternal in the sense that it is not temporal. It is outside time. (We shall see later that *eternal* and *everlasting* are not exact synonyms. *Everlasting* means what continues in time indefinitely, that is without ceasing. But eternity is outside time. It is a sphere of being in which everlastingness could never happen since it is beyond time.)

There can be no surprise that Christianity makes provision for punishment hereafter. As a religion of love, it could scarcely do otherwise. It would be astonishing, indeed outrageous to every moral scruple, if Christianity did *not* allow for eternal punishment. There is no room for the "good-heavens-what-have-we-here?" response to biblical texts which speak of torment in the hereafter. The omission of the teaching these texts give would certainly not leave us with a New Testament more easily accepted by people of humanity and decency.

It would, on the contrary, leave us with a message gravely inadequate to the demands of humanity and decency. After all, Christianity makes nonsense unless it reveals a system of being operative beyond time. A time-locked Christianity would be a contradiction in terms. In confronting Christianity, we are face to face with a religion which is supernaturally grounded beyond time and space. In confronting Christianity, we are face to face with a religion of love which makes a distinction between good and evil. In confronting Christianity, we are face to face with a religion whose values are to be fully explained and realized when earthly life is no more. For all these reasons it follows as the night follows the day that there must be a reckoning in the afterlife which will bring punishment to the wicked.

A central message of Christianity is that death is not the end. If it was not the end for Maximilian Kolbe and Anne Frank, then it was not the end for the Kaiser and Adolf Hitler. This has to be said because there seems to be a popular notion that for good people there is a life of peace and happiness awaiting them in the hereafter, but that death somehow finishes off the villains for good.

We may not actually *say* this. But we do say a good deal about the rest from tribulation which worthy souls must find when earthly life is o'er. We speak of how they have come home safe at last. We speak of how they are now reunited with their loved ones. Presumably we believe all this. We have it expensively inscribed on gravestones. But about the great villains we shrug our shoulders.

I suspect that there is something healthy about this contrast. We have no difficulty in thinking of our loved but lost relatives and of heroic and saintly souls of the past as living still. At the same time, we have real difficulty in picturing current existence for Hitler or Himmler. In their case the imagination has to close its eyes to the familiar vocabulary and imagery of rest and peace, joy and contentment, in a haven of tranquillity. On the other hand, medieval paintings of human beings roasted on spits, half submerged in quicksand, or bloodily dismembered and stumping around with their own severed heads in their hands, cannot be seriously entertained.

Certainly we find it difficult to picture jackbooted figures with swastikas on their armbands, their faces equipped with moustaches and pince-nez, screaming and writhing as they are prodded by devils. Yet it might be healthier to picture them like that, rather than to consign them to a state of untormented non-being. Indeed, it is something of an outrage to deal with them that way. Can we allow for the possibility that when Himmler's teeth closed on the phial hidden in his mouth and he dropped dead to the ground that that was the end of Heinrich Himmler? The end of thinking, knowing, feeling, and the beginning of what amounts to a blessed eternal sleep? Can we possibly imply that the arm of divine justice could reach no further than to grant this damaged and evil personality eternal rest at the age of forty-five?

I cannot read the obituary columns in the newspapers without noticing how many of our contemporaries presuppose a continuing life for their loved ones under divine protection. The good, the loved, the valued—it is assumed—live on. Then what about the villains? The question must be pressed again. Do they or do they not live on, too? If they do not live on, then on what basis of justice and love are they granted the blessing of release from all cares? And if they do live on, then where and how? The only alternative to the torment of a Dives is surely some final reconciliation.

It requires no forced stretching of the imagination to conceive of an eternal realm where a penitent murderer such as Myra Hindley meets her victims. Forgiveness is asked and forgiveness is granted. But what can we picture for Hitler or

Himmler? Must we try to imagine some grassy glade, all light and fragrant, where a long, long line files slowly forward so that each in turn can receive a personal apology from the Führer before clasping his hand in heartfelt forgiveness?

Or since it is easier for one person to get about than for several million, might it be better for the millions to stand massed in their countless formations, rank upon rank? Then we see the Führer—who is more accustomed to such proceedings—driven slowly past them in an angelically chauffeured convertible, his hand stretched out in reconciliation. That would be a rally to end all rallies! It just will not do. When we try to analyze what possible alternative future there could be for someone like this, we see how decisively logic and justice demand penalty as well as reward in the hereafter.

Life's Loose Ends

The Christian believes that our life on earth derives its purpose and its meaning from the supernatural. God made the world and its creatures. He made them with a purpose. And when his creatures went astray his own Son suffered and died to restore them to their inheritance. Our lives here thus draw their meaning from the way we are involved in the great drama of creation and redemption.

In other words, we should not expect things to make sense for us in all respects if we only view them from the limited perspective of our earthly lives. What we are involved in here and now takes its true motivation and purpose from the drama that starts in eternity and ends in eternity. What happens within our short lifespans is not meant to be complete and conclusive.

Let me tell you the story of a couple whom I will call John and Agnes. The story begins with the arrival of Agnes in England to study. The daughter of an American doctor and his wife, she came to a British university where she met John, and the two fell in love. John is an Englishman. It is a conventional enough story to begin with. John got a good job in the insurance world, and the couple were married. They had two children at school when the blow fell. Agnes was stricken with multiple sclerosis.

The disease progressed rapidly and soon Agnes was confined to a wheelchair. John responded heroically. His occupation allowed him a certain amount of control over his own working hours. He managed to do his job properly, to care for his children, to comfort his wife, and to keep the home functioning. This was not done without some help. But when Agnes's parents came over from the United States to see what they could do for their afflicted daughter they were appalled. It was not just the tragedy of Agnes's condition that appalled them, but the price her husband was paying. John loved his wife dearly and never grumbled. But the parents worked on Agnes, persuading her that it was her duty to free her husband from what they saw as the ruination of his life.

What were their motives? In the first place, in the medical profession themselves, they believed that by taking their daughter back to the United States they could make better provision for her treatment and supply more sophisticated aids to help her to cope with her condition. In the second place, they could not bear to see their son-in-law so burdened by their own daughter. There was perhaps an element of injured pride here.

They felt themselves responsible. They had money. They could whisk their daughter away to where her own medical needs could be answered, while the weight was lifted from her own mind of knowing that she was a burden to her beloved husband. A divorce would enable him to make a new start. John loved his wife and did not want to be divorced. Agnes loved her husband. Only under pressure did she decide to divorce him.

This part of John's story is known to the writer, but I lack intimacy of acquaintance to clarify all of the details. Enough is known anyway to make clear that for John and Agnes there is a heartrending incompleteness about their marriage and about their lives. John's in-laws, who have plenty of resources, persuaded him to let them take his two children to the United States at least for the present where they will certainly be well cared for. A wife has parted with her husband out of unselfish concern for his welfare. A father has parted with his children out of unselfish concern for their welfare. A divorce has been sought by a wife out of love for her husband.

John's life story is not over. But whatever happens there are some loose ends which will never be tied up here below. There can never be a meaningful conclusion to the story of his marriage this side the grave. His case points to the fact that it is only in a life hereafter that the untidinesses of earthly life can be cleared up.

Untidinesses may seem like a very inadequate word to describe emotional plights such as John's. But the line of argument here is that it is *not* only acts of wickedness and evil that leave loose ends in the pattern of things when viewed with the eyes of love. Though much more will need to be said on this matter when we turn to consider heaven rather than hell, the point to be stressed is that life within time can be judged as meaningful only in relation to what ultimately happens outside time. At the earthly level even the exercise of love may cause great damage. At the earthly level the pressures of sympathetic unselfishness may actually destroy in the very process of seeking to heal.

Our lives abound all too often in what is painfully inconclusive. Relationships are botched up. Worthy attempts to right them are foiled. Aspirations are shattered. Christians come to terms with this by recognizing that earthly life is not the sum total of things. It would be intolerable to conceive of an eternal existence which, instead of filling out life's inadequacies, actually compounded them. An eternity which renders life's broken and random experiences meaningful is a tenable concept. An eternity which outdoes time in producing experiences that are irreconcilable with meaningfulness and purpose is an absurd notion. To entertain the idea would involve positing a first cause of things which is indifferent if not malevolent.

What has been put here in abstract terms might be better expressed concretely. When a man dies, he will surely find life's tangled issues clarified in the light of eternity. He will surely learn where he has done well and where he has done ill. There may be surprises for him on this score. No doubt there will be. But nothing like the surprise there would be for him to learn that nothing was going to be clarified for the simple reason that it did not matter after all.

Yet if there is no eternal reckoning for the wicked, does not that amount to a public declaration that in the long run the issue of good and evil does not matter after all? Picture a heavenly reception on such terms. "You thought it mattered? You struggled to do your best? You fought a long fight with the temptation to be mean to your intolerably overbearing mother-in-law? You prayed desperately about it, and you managed to control yourself. You were lured into excessive drinking, but you struggled against that, too. You prayed for strength and you conquered the habit. Fine. Now let me introduce you to your opposite number here, who can make no such claim, can you, Roger?

"No, Roger never dreamed for a moment that it mattered. He never thought about anyone's interests but his own. He worshiped himself, you might say. Anything that came his way that seemed worth having he grabbed with both hands and to hell with anyone else. He killed himself with drink. He just about finished off his wife. Anyway, that's all in the past. I think you two ought to get to know each other. You're such different types. You'll have a lot to talk about. It takes all sorts to make an eternity. We're all equal here."

The Christian cannot tolerate the idea of an afterlife which reinforces the injustices of earthly life instead of correcting them and prolongs the moral confusions of earthly life instead of clearing them up. There is no such thing as a conceivable time-eternity relationship between what is meaningless or at best half-meaningful and what is fully meaningful—between what is fragmentary and what is complete—between what is inconclusive and what is resolved.

We have seen how death leaves human pilgrimages littered with what is meaningless, fragmentary, and inconclusive. It is not difficult to picture an afterlife for unselfish and generous people in which these loose ends are gathered together and knitted into a pattern. But this chapter is not primarily concerned with what an afterlife has in store for the virtuous. It is concerned with what an afterlife has in store for those who remain cruel or self-centered to the end.

There are only three logical possibilities for such people at death. They may enter a state of happiness. They may enter a state of punishment. Or they may enter a state of oblivion. The rubber stamp of total oblivion resolves nothing. It merely confirms what has been meaningless in their earthly careers as meaningless, what has been fragmentary as fragmentary, what has been inconclusive as inconclusive.

"You made your living, and a rich one too, by organizing the shipment of heroin from Pakistan to Europe. Your agents hooked dropouts and hard cases. You then made supply conditional on their pushing drugs to others. Yours was a life of calculated and sustained injury to the bodies and souls of many of your fellow creatures. There are thousands who have scores to settle with you—your victims, the parents of your victims, and many others.

"However, that doesn't matter any more. We have a little phial of spiritual cyanide for you. Once you take it, it will be as though you had never been born." What wonderful news. No more consciousness. No question of ever having to meet any of those whose lives you have damaged. No spectacles of misery and degradation to be forced on you with the compelling knowledge, "This was your doing."

In any conceivable scheme of things which makes sense of the created order, the damage done by evil must be brought home to its perpetrators. This is both a moral and a rational necessity. Assume a design and purpose in the created order, and that is a minimal requirement. Only in a system bred by chance and developed by chance could there be a situation where what is meaningless is never given meaning. Only in such a system could the wicked commit evil and never meet their own faces in the mirror of judgment.

Moral consciousness has given human beings the ability to distinguish between good and evil. Our moral consciousness presupposes a point of clarification at which all good is known as good and all evil is exposed as evil. It is the moral awareness of good and evil that enables us to evaluate our experience and judge the activities of our fellow human beings.

When you say of an act "That is mean" or "That is generous," when you say of an act "That was brutal" or "That was compassionate," when you say of an attitude "That is hostile" or "That is friendly," you are differentiating between good and evil. And if you analyze your own thinking, you will recognize that you have at least a vague notion of how this distinguishes where human beings are headed along the road of earthly life.

They are going somewhere—or they are going somewhere else. But if they are all going the same way—or rather if no one is going anywhere at all, then moral consciousness itself is an absurdity.

I have done no more in this chapter than attempt to suggest that most considerations of the doctrine of hell start at the wrong end. "The New Testament teaches a religion of love," writers tell us, "but good heavens what have we here? A threat of eternal torment for wicked men and women. How can we reconcile that with a God of love?" The "good-heavens-what-have-we-here?" approach is illogical. I suggest that if we start not from some mistily conceived abstraction of God's love but from the concrete realities of our experience on this planet, we shall realize that hell is necessary.

It comes down to this. All that causes injustice or affliction is no doubt to be expected in this life if human history is evolving by chance under neither God's initiation nor his direction. But if life in time is contained within a life in eternity where a Creator dwells, then we should expect something else. If, as every Christian believes, God created everything and controls our destiny here, then the sum total of what I have called loose ends cannot possibly be final. And if it is not final, then truth must clarify the human pilgrimage under the eye of love. And that will inevitably involve punishment for wrongdoing. The length of punishment cannot be logically measured in a state of being to which time itself does not apply. But punishment itself is inevitable if we presuppose that God's truth will clarify and tidy up life's loose ends.

TWO

The Alternative to Salvation

Rejecting Salvation

Christianity is a religion of redemption and salvation. Redemption from what? Salvation from what? As an instructed Christian you will reply, "Redemption from sin, from the bondage of sin." Talk of redeeming people and saving people cannot make sense unless we know what captivity they are being redeemed from, what ills they are being saved from. It is this, the great Alternative to redemption and salvation in Christ, that we are concerned with here.

John the Baptist came preaching repentance for "the kingdom of heaven is at hand." The kingdom of heaven is clearly a pleasant state to be a subject of, but what is the alternative? In what state are we left if we refuse to repent and enter the kingdom? Again, as an instructed Christian, you will reply, "The alternative to the kingdom of heaven is the kingdom of this world. Our Lord made the choice between the two quite clear."

Now that sounds straightforward enough. We have a choice between the kingdom of heaven and the kingdom of this world, between serving God and serving mammon or the things of this world. The idealist will not have difficulty in stating his preference. But we are not all idealists, and some people seem to make a pretty good thing out of choosing the kingdom of this world and undeviating devotion to mammon.

Indeed the psalms are full of complaints that the unrighteous flourish. Yet when John the Baptist appears on the scene the urgency of his message implies a terrible destiny for those who refuse to hear and repent. This urgency is evident throughout our Lord's teaching and it has been evident ever since in the teaching of his disciples.

Now you can appeal urgently to others to accept an offer of salvation only if what they are to be saved from is dire. If you call out the fire brigade to your neighbor's house so that the place is soon surrounded by rising ladders and the street festooned with fire hoses, you will be accused of gross flippancy and irresponsibility should it turn out that the reason for your call was that you saw through the window a candle burning on a table. Firemen stretching out a blanket urging a woman to jump into it from an upstairs window would be judged unfit for their jobs if there were no flames leaping up from below and the only glow through a downstairs window were that of a table lamp or a candle.

Our Lord himself made clear that the alternative to salvation was dire. When he was asked about some recent calamities—the Galileans slaughtered by Pilate and the eighteen victims killed by the tower falling on them at Siloam—he made clear that these disasters were not specific instances of divine punishment imposed on notably guilty sinners. He warned that his listeners would share just such a tragic fate if they did not repent (Lk 13:5).

Was our Lord crying wolf?

We are called upon to jump from the upstairs window into the saving arms of firemen. But are we quite sure that the house is on fire beneath us? Those people in the downstairs apartment do not seem to have left. The divine fire brigade has gathered in the street below. The hose of grace is hurling a stream of lifegiving water into the air. The jet of spray is pounding at our walls, and it is all but blinding us. The fire chief calls upon us once more to jump to safety. Perhaps we'd better finally take the advice of the divine brigade. So we jump into the saving arms poised below. We are slightly injured in the fall and we suffer shock.

Reflecting on it all next day in our hospital bed, we are surprised to receive a visit from Jack W. Wiseman who lives in the apartment beneath us. "There was never really any danger, you know. The fat caught fire in my frying pan. I couldn't put it out, so I threw the blazing pan out of the kitchen window. I don't know what the fire brigade thought they were doing. Did you get badly hurt?"

How do they fare, those who jump and those who don't? Let us consider two cases I have personally come across.

There is Rosemary Danby. She had a strong-minded father who died young when she was a girl of fourteen. She had an ailing mother who eventually became something of a burden to her only daughter. Rosemary is not unintelligent. But between an overly dominant father and a rather limply acquiescent mother, she somehow failed to achieve enough self-confidence to cope satisfactorily with a career. Her father had not thought self-confidence an appropriate characteristic for a daughter. Her mother had lost interest in cultivating a quality she considered so abrasively unsettling to domestic tranquillity. Rosemary early on tended to retreat into lone activities, and she acquired considerable skill as a pianist.

Unfortunately, her lack of self-confidence was such that she could play effectively only when she believed no one else was listening. Her musical skill was rendered useless as a means of playing a part in social life. The need to make a living led her to train to be a teacher. But when classroom realities had to be faced on her own, she found herself unable to cope. She had a breakdown. She suffered great unhappiness. Yet she had had a religious upbringing, and at the crisis point in her life she jumped out of her misery into the saving arms of the Lord.

The story does not have a blissfully happy ending. Rosemary cannot now be said to be a bustling career woman running a thriving business. The Lord's miracles are not of that kind. She will never make speeches on platforms or at garden parties. She will always be rather reticent, unassertive, tentative, and self-deprecatory. But she has a firm faith. She is a woman of prayer. She has put her trust in God, and he will not fail her. The human drama of her life which looked like turning into tragedy did not in the final denouement turn into a sunny lighthearted comedy. But it became ultimately a steady pilgrimage lived in fortitude and some degree of cheerfulness.

Surely we can all point to cases we have known and say, "There is a man or there is a woman who was saved from despair by commitment to Christ." We have seen cases and we have read of cases where some utterly destructive habit or addiction had a man or a woman in its grip. The leap of faith was made, the commitment was held on to, and a life of increasing misery became a life of sobriety and steadiness lived in quiet discipleship.

We know of these cases, and they enable us to answer the question, "Was our Lord crying wolf?" with a decisive "No." They help us answer the question, "What is the alternative to repentance and entry into the kingdom?" with clear answers. The alternative was rapid progress toward deteriorating health and eventually death. The alternative was an eventual charge of embezzlement and ten years in prison. The alternative was despair and eventual insanity.

The skeptic would say at this point that I have been very selective in giving an example of human response to Christ's call where the alternative could be said to be truly dire. But there is no intention here to load the argument. Let us consider another person whose career has come to my notice.

Terence Whelpam was born into a good family with social status, enough resources to ensure comfort, and a distinctive position in the cultural world. His parents mixed with people of some achievement in the spheres of art, literature, and scholarship. The circle, however, was rather bohemian than aristocratic in its way of life, rather progressive and radical than conservative in its thinking. Terence took to the *liberated* notions of the early twentieth century anti-Victorian enlightenment. Free love was fashionable. The political and social establishments were regarded as rather absurd. Religion was a laughably outmoded restriction on healthy appetites, especially the sexual appetites, of noble natural men and women.

Terence was a confirmed atheist, happy to ridicule believers. He insisted on the absurdity of lifelong monogamy and the delights of promiscuity. Amiability of character seems to have been one of his assets since all his friends called him Toby, speaking of him as though he were a pet dog that was nice to have around.

There is no need to go into the details of Terence's marriages. He openly derided fidelity. He openly celebrated the pleasures of sex with various partners. He wrote books. In some of them he did his best to indoctrinate others into his own moral anarchism. He had a seemingly happy life. He lived well, sometimes in England, sometimes on the continent. He was handsome enough to be able to attract the women he wanted.

With his schooling and his reading he could not but be aware of what Christian revelation was all about, and he could not be less interested. He enjoyed good health. He was something of a connoisseur of good food and wine. He was cheerful. He lived to the ripe old age of eighty-seven. He died peacefully in his bed.

So what, for Terence, was the dire alternative to responding to Christ's call to repent, to believe, and to enter the kingdom of heaven? A comfortable home, a seemingly trouble-free life, a liberal supply of attractive mistresses, a good cellar, a circle of intelligent friends, lifelong enjoyment of reading, the success of publication, the satisfaction of enjoying a certain celebrity status, long years passed in enjoyable work and enjoyable pleasures. What more could Terence have asked for out of life?

Now you may ask, did I know Terence well enough to be sure that there was no inner canker eating away at his peace of mind? Was there perhaps a dawning sense in his later years of a spiritual void opening up around him? No, I did not know enough of him to swear that his composure remained true to form to the bitter end. But if he had any doubts at all about the rightness of his atheistic pursuit of life's pleasures, he certainly concealed them well. The words that came from his pen and the face that appeared in the newspapers and on the bookjackets told the same story that I have told. He had chosen the great Alternative. And he had done very well, thank you.

So where does that leave our argument? The cynic might say that we have made a good case that the saving arms of our Lord and the kingdom of heaven are a welcome alternative to a life of increasing despair for a nervous woman like Rosemary. But it follows that the saving arms of God and the kingdom of heaven would make an unnecessary and thoroughly unwelcome alternative to a life of robust self-indulgence by an immoral atheist like Terence.

There is small need to press home our conclusion. It is simply that when one asks the questions, "What does redemption redeem us from?" and "What does salvation save us from?" we see that no thoroughly satisfactory answer can be provided merely in terms of earthly life. If the dire consequences of not believing and not repenting are to be taken seriously—as surely our Lord leaves us in no doubt that they are—then those dire consequences cannot be firmly located in time. The dire consequences *must* be eternal.

Dives and Lazarus

Our Lord's story of Dives and Lazarus makes this point (Lk 16:19-31). The rich man who has had little time for the poverty-stricken beggar, Lazarus, at his gate, lifts up his eyes in torment in hell and begs Abraham to send the beggar to him to moisten his parched lips with water. Lazarus had wanted the crumbs from the rich man's table, a very modest requirement for unwanted leftovers such as might be fed to animals. After death the rich man begs a comparably modest favor. Yet being reduced like Lazarus to collecting or receiving uneaten morsels in a doggie bag is a rather servile state. On the other hand, dipping your fingers in water to moisten a man's mouth is an act of comfort and condescension more befitting a nurse than a beggar.

So the reversal of roles is a violent one. It is sharpened further by the fact that an unsavory creature lying at the gate with dogs licking his sores is not the first person whose moistened fingers a man accustomed to be clad in purple and fine linen would want on his lips. However, Abraham's rejection of the rich man's request has a twofold basis. "Son, remember that thou in thy lifetime receivedst thy good things, and likewise Lazarus evil things: but now he is comforted, and thou art tormented" (Lk 16:25).

The first reason is quite simply that Dives has had more of his share of good things on earth, and Lazarus much less than his share. The afterlife apparently exists to counterbalance this inequality.

And the second reason for Abraham's rejection of the rich man's request is: "And beside all this, between us and you there is a great gulf fixed: so that they which would pass from hence to you cannot; neither can they pass to us, that would come from thence" (Lk 16:26). The crossing of the gulf between heaven and hell is impossible. This is one of the most sobering and frightening sentences in the New Testament.

The balance of event and argument in this story is quite remarkable. Abraham does not tell Dives that he has been a selfish, mean, unloving fellow and must expect his punishment. Indeed, our Lord lays the emphasis not on punishing selfishness but on correcting the earthly balance sheet of well-being and deprivation. We might reasonably assume that the punishment of greed and selfishness is an implicit theme.

Nevertheless, that theme is not pressed home. Our Lord seems to have had other lessons in mind. The seeming injustices and inequalities of earthly life are going to be corrected, and that is what the other life is in part about. Secondly the emphasis is on the impassable gulf between heaven and hell. We see the utter impossibility of recanting on the one hand or of going to the aid of the condemned on the other hand. Above all else, there is the hard fact that there is *no* second chance. The all-important message seems to be a dire warning to all who think they can get away with things in earthly life.

The plight of Dives is certainly grave. Not only is he refused a drink of water to alleviate his torment, he is also sharply rebuffed. In a surprising show of seemingly unselfish concern for others, he begs that some warning should be sent to his brothers of what is in store for them if they continue to live as he himself lived. Father Abraham's rebuff is uncompromising. "Your brothers have had all the usual advantages of living in a society where God's word was taught, and they took no notice. There would be no point in making a special appeal to people so deaf to what they have been taught by God's prophets." This cuts near the bone.

Terence Whelpam and his like were brought up in an environment where the Christian faith was preached week by week in churches and chapels that were easily accessible. He became acquainted with the Bible at school. However atheistic and pleasure-loving the immediate environment of his family circle may have been, Terence could not but be conscious of the way of life based on acceptance of Christian revelation which many of his contemporaries followed. In fact, a key element in Terence's upbringing was that his parents' circle represented a peculiar minority making a radical challenge to prevalently accepted values and beliefs, especially to the upholders of traditional Christian moral and doctrinal teaching. In his novels, Terence did not hesitate to portray clergymen as figures of pathetic absurdity.

Let us look at Terence's career of happy enmity to God in the light of the parable of Dives and Lazarus. Then perhaps it will no longer surprise us that his happiness was seemingly unruffled, that apparently no event caused him to question his selfish philosophy, and that no grief or suffering so devastated him that he was thrown to his knees in prayer.

The message in Scripture about the hereafter appears to be: "He has Moses and the prophets. He has the parish church at the end of the street. He hears God's word spoken when he attends church for a funeral or a wedding. The odd Christian whom he comes across makes an occasional remark which would cause a sensitive man to cast a thought in the direction of those spiritual things which he ignores. Inevitably, his reading of past literature often leads him into the intellectual company of earnest, faithful, instructed Christians. He pays no attention to these people. Why *should we expect* him to pay attention if a special word was directed to him individually from beyond time?"

Why indeed! We have all known people and heard of others whose lives have been beneficially transformed as a result of some remarkable revelation or some crushing blow. I know of a bishop whose spiritual life acquired a new depth, his teaching a new urgency, and his pastoral care a new charisma after his only son was tragically killed. God chose *not* to kill off one of Terence's children prematurely in a road accident. Perhaps he knew that the sacrifice would be in vain. For Terence's first wife died early of cancer and the event made no deep impression on him spiritually or even intellectually. He was so opposed to monogamy in principle and so open to promiscuity in practice that loss of a wife could scarcely be reckoned a threat to his earthly well-being.

We have to confess that we do not like the uncompromising rebuff to Dives at the point where he seems to be wanting to help someone else. His request sounds like an impulse towards amendment. It implies a recognition that he made the wrong choice himself and then, disinterestedly it seems, conveys a desire to prevent others from making the same mistake. We don't like to think that it is too late for any human creature to mend his ways. We feel that Father Abraham is being very unforgiving. So we have to remind ourselves that after all Dives has finished his earthly life and is receiving his eternal punishment.

Now whatever eternal punishment is like, one thing is surely indisputable, it must be effective. Ineffective punishment could scarcely have a place in a divinely ordained system. And if punishment is effective it makes the punished one aware of why he is being punished and what it is that is being paid for. Therefore, difficult as it may be for us to conceive of the thoughts of one undergoing eternal punishment, regret for what has produced the punishment must certainly have a place.

"I wish I hadn't neglected the poor man at the gate" is not an impulse towards amendment or contrition. It is merely a rationalization of "I wish I were not here in hell, suffering these torments." It is not greater concern for the Lazaruses of this world that changes the attitude of Dives, it is the pains of hell. In short, the thought of suffering beggars lying in the street with dogs licking their sores could not on earth and, so far as we can see, cannot now in hell affect Dives. For him what was wrong about neglecting Lazarus was that it bought him a ticket to hell through the irreversible turnstile.

What about the other aspect of Dives's request, the seeming concern for his brothers? Here the point of Abraham's rebuff is not difficult to distinguish from the superficial appearance of being unforgiving. The brothers "have Moses and the prophets." What Dives wants for his brothers is a messenger to earth from the hereafter confirming the reality of hell. The proposal seems to be that Lazarus, the known beggar, should return to earth bearing about him all the marks of his newfound bliss and give a firsthand account of Dives's condition. Then, taking note of the way the tables have been turned on rich man and beggar, the brothers will conclude that the game is up and they need to mend their ways.

Dives clearly wants incontrovertible evidence of the here-after to be conveyed to the living. We may observe that if firsthand evidence of hell's torments were to be flashed on our television screens like pictures of the landing on the moon, then human freedom would be no more. Abraham does not make this point, for our Lord had a more personal and immediate concern to convey to his hearers: "If they hear not Moses and the prophets, neither will they be persuaded, though one rose from the dead" (Lk 16:31).

Those who ignore the teaching of the prophets are not going to be impressed by anything Christ may do. Rising from the dead in corroboration of the teaching of Moses and the prophets may be the clinching revelation for some. But the brothers of Dives, like Terence, would remain unpersuaded.

Yet the balance sheet of the eternal life of Dives and Lazarus still tugs at our hearts. We exist in a society where the Christian message has been widely sentimentalized into a posture of unlimited forgiveness and indiscriminate indulgence. Now it is true that we are urged to be ready to forgive our brothers not once or twice but unto seventy times seven. But forgiveness presupposes repentance. And those who would think of God as a fount of mercy showering indulgence on every wrong cannot possibly justify their view biblically. The more we study the Bible, the more we shall be struck by the theme of payment, a theme which is in line with the balance sheet of the eternal lot of Dives and Lazarus.

The very notion of redemption has to do with paying a price which will ransom prisoners from their captivity. The price paid in Christ's suffering on the cross is so unspeakably vast that the mind is overwhelmed in any attempt to conceive the character and scope of the captivity which could make necessary such a ransom price. Why does God authorize an expenditure so costly as that of his own son's lifeblood? Why does he not smile down paternally on the creatures he has made and wash all their troubles away in a flash?

Now you may say that it is the enormity of human sin that calls out a compensating divine act of such tremendous magnitude. Indeed! And suppose I ask you to specify what you mean by human sin. You mean murder, theft, rape, acts of hatred, brutality, and greed? Yes, and more than that, for in a sense these are all subsidiary sins deriving from our failure to keep the two most crucial commandments.

When Jesus was asked which is the great commandment in the law, he replied:

> Thou shalt love the Lord thy God with all thy heart, and with all thy soul, and with all thy mind. This is the first and great commandment. And the second is like unto it, Thou shalt love thy neighbor as thyself. On these two commandments hang all the law and the prophets. (Mt 22:37-40)

If the love of God is the first of all obligations laid on us, then I can see that Terence Whelpam was a non-starter in the good life. His friends may have fondly showed their liking for him by calling him Toby, but he had no liking at all for God. Christ, the Son of God, died in agony on the cross for us. And when Rosemary Danby turned to God in prayer and supplication out of the depths of her inadequacy and her despair, the Lord heard her voice. She was comforted and sustained. We can see what door was opened to the divine mercy by the divine and human suffering of Christ. But again, what about Terence Whelpam, whose rejection of God opened the door to a Mediterranean villa with coffee at eleven and vintage claret for dinner? What about the Porsche at the door and the richly furnished bedroom upstairs for the reception of his successive mistresses?

God is not mocked, we are told. But this would indeed be mockery of God if there were no accounting beyond the grave. The presence and poise, the smile and self-satisfaction of Terence Whelpam constituted a cornering of shares in unearned happiness that the final audit will not conceivably overlook.

There are varying degrees of literalness in our Lord's teaching. Clearly when he instructed directly, especially in response to a specific question such as "Which is the great commandment in the law?" then he taught plainly and comprehensively. You must love God with all your heart and soul and mind. And you must love your neighbor as yourself. There can be no argument here about what Christ meant. But when he told a parable like the story of Dives and Lazarus, he sought not to give comprehensive instruction about the whole way of life but to stress one or two points in particular.

It may be all-important to love God first, but there is no mention about whether Dives made any effort to love God or to perform any religious duties. Plainly he did not love his neighbor as himself. He left his neighbor lying in the road at his gate sick and hungry, and he did nothing about it. However, not even this point is made specifically. All we are told of Dives is that he wore expensive clothes and "fared sumptuously everyday." The rest we have to deduce.

We are reluctant to conclude that a man can be condemned to hellfire simply because he dresses well and eats well; although "faring sumptuously every day" does suggest to us a regular routine of seven-course dinners washed down with bottles of vintage Chablis and Mouton-Rothschild. But what is important is that the sins of Dives appear to have been what we call sins of omission. It was what he didn't do rather than what he did do which brought judgment down upon him. Presumably God's attitude to his expensive suits would have been different if he had equipped Lazarus with a spare one of comparable quality. And his attitude to Dives's sumptuous menus would have been different *if* he had invited Lazarus to partake at his side.

The Parable of the Judgment

In his direct forecast of the judgment (Mt 25:31-46), our Lord's whole emphasis is upon sins of omission. The Son of Man will come in glory and will sit in judgment upon all the nations gathered before him. They will be divided into sheep and goats: the sheep on the right hand, the goats on the left hand. Those on the right hand are the "blessed of the Father" and they are called in to "inherit the kingdom." Those on the left hand are "cursed" instead of "blessed." They are ordered to depart "into everlasting fire prepared for the devil and his angels." On these terms it is clear that the examination we are submitted to at the end of our earthly pilgrimage is an old-fashioned, no-nonsense test. We either flunk or we pass. No cases are going to be deferred for further consideration. Our Lord says to those who are condemned:

> For I was ahungered, and ye gave me no meat: I was thirsty, and ye gave me no drink: I was a stranger, and ye took me not in: naked, and ye clothed me not: sick, and in prison, and ye visited me not. (Mt 25:42-43)

The condemned souls are bewildered by what Jesus has just told them. When did we treat you like that? they ask him. And our Lord tells them: "Inasmuch as ye did it not to one of the least of these, ye did it not to me" (Mt 25:45).

Of the five failures mentioned, four of them are the failures of Dives. He failed to give food or drink, shelter or clothing to Lazarus. And the whole multitude who shared his sins of omission are condemned to the flames. There are no half measures. No one is allowed to plead plaintively that he once gave a sandwich to a tramp and once gave an old overcoat to a charity shop, so could he please be allowed to try again at the prison-visiting bit? It is a discouraging scene for most of us.

No one is accused of wife-beating or assault. No one is accused of child abuse or blackmail. No one is charged with *any* aggressively brutal or savage act. Not a single committed sin is referred to. Awful thoughts strike us. It may have been even on the way to church that one of the condemned regularly passed the prison gates yet never stepped in to console an inmate. Another of the condemned may have been reading his Bible, or even writing a religious book, when he glimpsed through the window a filthy tramp struggling up the garden path. Apprehensive lest his important religious work be interrupted, he is relieved to hear his wife go to the door and salve his conscience by giving the fellow a handful of change.

Another of the condemned may have been too busy wrapping Christmas presents for his friends and working on the church accounts for the annual audit to have time to call on the neighbor who had cut off some toes with an electric saw. These are indeed disturbing thoughts. For it is surely most likely to be the one who has been busily and, as we like to say, healthily occupied who would be most likely to say to the Son of Man on Judgment day, "Wait a minute! When did I treat you like that?" And presumably the reply will be, "Inasmuch as you passed the prison gates regularly on your way to church and never thought of going in to comfort an inmate, you ignored me. Inasmuch as you immersed yourself in theological argument when a tramp was at the door in need, you ignored me. Inasmuch as you were too preoccupied to call on an injured neighbor, you ignored me."

On this basis it seems appallingly easy to run up a debit account with God. While we are busy with this worthwhile work or that, while we are active in the social or liturgical life of our church, even while we are about our daily prayers, there are hungry fellow beings, inadequately clothed and sheltered, fellow beings, sick and imprisoned fellow beings, suffering from precisely the neglect which our own preoccupations exemplify. While we are looking the other way, what is happening behind our backs is after all going to determine whether we are to be eternally classified with the sheep or the goats.

Is it really as bad as that? Perhaps it isn't. For after all there is much in our Lord's teaching which promises salvation on rather different terms from those which involve a perpetual scurrying here and there on missions of charity to people less fortunate than ourselves. But such promises of salvation are not what this chapter is about. This chapter is concerned with the great Alternative to salvation, with the destiny promised by our Lord for those who fail the test.

In fact, our Lord's picture of dividing the sheep from the goats is not wholly depressing. It is not only the condemned who are bewildered by what is attributed to them. The saved are bewildered, too. "You gave me food and drink when I was hungry and thirsty. You gave me shelter and clothing when I was homeless and cold. You visited me when I was sick or in prison."

The righteous want to know what this is all about. It has to be spelled out to them that when they served the needs of the needy they ministered to Christ. It is a pleasing corollary. If your unintended neglect of our Lord can catch up with you, your unintended service to our Lord can catch up with you, too. If damnation by default seems a dismal possibility opened up by this vision of judgment, salvation as an unanticipated bonus for voluntary welfare work has the happy acceptability of an unearned increment.

We must be careful not to press the moral of any of our Lord's parables or stories to a general conclusion which its particular message cannot support. If we want his comprehensive message, we must turn to his comprehensive statements. You must love God with all your heart and mind, and you must love your neighbor as yourself. If these are the crucial first principles for human lives, if these are the linchpins of all morality, if the serving of these purposes is precisely the end for which man was created, then there is a logical deduction which is inescapable. Man's failure to love God with all his heart and mind, and man's failure to love his neighbor as himself are together the attitudes which upset the whole applecart of God's purpose for us.

And if these two failures are the attitudes which put awry the whole providential scheme for the human race, then these two failures are precisely those evils that are of such magnitude that they justified and justify the costliest of all expenditures,

Christ's death on the cross. It is not surprising then that at the judgment our Lord divides the sheep from the goats on the basis of the love they have shown for their fellow creatures. For this is the lower threshold of the two that would cause the wicked to stumble.

A man who cannot love the brother he has seen can certainly not love the God whom he has not seen. That is the apostle John's summary of the matter in his first letter: "And this commandment have we from him, That he who loveth God love his brother also" (1 Jn 4:21).

We see that Jesus scarcely needed to tackle the question of the religious life in picturing the judgment for those who are condemned. They had not loved their neighbors. They could not possibly have loved God. For them, judgment need go no further.

Earthly Punishment

"The kingdom of God is within you," our Lord told his disciples (Lk 17:21). Might he have said to those who rejected him, "The state of hell is within you?" If this life offers us at times a foretaste of heaven, does it also offer us a foretaste of hell? We have considered cases like that of Dives and that of Terence Whelpam who, it appears, never for a moment asked themselves whether their attitude and their way of life might be piling up an immense debit in the divine ledger which would have to be painfully accounted for in the hereafter.

But there is surely a good deal in our experience and certainly a good deal in the record of literature and of history which shows people paying dearly for their misdeeds while still on earth. If, as we have seen, punishment in hell must inevitably involve consciousness of having brought misery upon oneself and regret for having done so, then that is certainly not an experience peculiar to the afterlife. In that respect we have all had our taste of hell on earth. And indeed, even without reference to the Christian gospel, life is so ordered by divine providence that no intelligent human being can fail to learn from his experience that the following principle operates: You may choose A or B; but if you choose B, you will pay for it. That is a mark of our human situation in time.

If you eat too much you will get indigestion. If you persistently eat too much you will put on weight and your body will become a burden to you. If you drink too much you will get a headache and eventually a hangover. If you persistently drink too much you will develop cirrhosis of the liver and delirium tremens. If you are sexually promiscuous and visit prostitutes, you may well get syphilis or gonorrhea. If you indulge in homosexual perversions, you are quite likely to contract AIDS. There are certain penalties built into the course of human life.

These penalties are not always physical. It has generally been assumed that a murderer would pay for his crime by inner mental torment even if he were never found out. One of the great successes of the Victorian theater was the extraordinary melodrama *The Bells* by Leopold Lewis, a play in which for thirty-five years Henry Irving captivated audiences in the role of Mathias, the burgomaster of a village in the Alsace region. Fifteen years after murdering a travelling Jewish merchant from Poland for his gold, Mathias is a well-to-do, respected man with municipal honors. But he has never been able to shake off the terrible memory of the night when the Jew's horse, bells ringing round its neck, drew its master on a sleigh through the snow.

Mathias crept up behind him, felled him with an axe, and then carried the corpse to a limekiln. Ringing bells haunt the guilty man, forever renewing the vision of the crime in his mind and indeed before his eyes. It is obviously appropriate to speak of such a person as experiencing a hell on earth.

Literature is full of such testimonies to the mental penalty one usually pays for murder. When Macbeth weighs the pros and cons of assassinating Duncan he is prepared to thrust the possibility of punishment after death from his mind. He is more worried that "we still have judgment here," that bloody crimes are apt to rebound on those who commit them. And as murder succeeds to murder, he is so shaken night by night with terrible dreams that he begins to envy the peace of death to which his dagger has dispatched his first victim.

Man is divinely endowed with a conscience and one of its functions seems to be to warn him in advance what hell is like. That the voice of conscience can be thoroughly suppressed we know. If Hitler or Himmler suffered from sleeplessness, we may doubt whether it was on account of the screams and smells which rose from the battlefields and gas chambers. But we do not regard such seeming monsters of iniquity as characteristic of the human race.

In civilized Christendom one function of the law has been to corroborate the voice of conscience and give it authoritative support. The law, we may say, is the public conscience equipped with teeth. Thus if you murder or steal, damage another by violence or by slander, the forces of the law will do their best to punish you. In one sense, therefore, the law is a means of restraining by threat of punishment human urges which might otherwise result in criminality.

This is what we mean when we say that the law gives the public conscience teeth. It is the morally weak who derive the greatest benefit from the law's teeth. The virtuous man would refrain from murder and theft even if they were not criminal offenses. The Christian who is aware of the threat of eternal punishment does not need to be deterred from sins by the threat of a few months in jail.

The function of the law in protecting the morally weak against themselves has been crucial in Christendom. This point is made because in recent decades the notion that the law exists only to protect one person from another rather than any person from himself has produced profound changes in legislation and in public attitudes. It must be understood that when we speak of the law in this context we refer not only to the formal regulations which, if broken, bring criminal charges into play. We also mean the informal, tacitly understood protocols and etiquettes which govern family and social relationships.

Thus, though there has been no formal law against adultery in our countries, there was until recently an accepted code which turned it into an offense against respectability. In this sense the informal, tacit codes have functioned like law to strengthen the morally weak against themselves. The destruction of such informal codes in recent decades—together with the abolition of restrictive legislation against such practices as homosexuality and abortion—has knocked the teeth out of the public conscience. So too have changes in the law and changes in attitude toward divorce.

I have just read an article in *The Times* (London) noting that divorce figures in the United Kingdom have risen by a further eleven percent, since recent changes in the law have allowed couples to petition for divorce after one year of marriage instead of three. The estimated proportion of marriages ending in divorce has gone up from two percent in 1911 to thirty-three percent in 1986. So-called progressive politicians urge that divorce proceedings should be allowed even earlier. They stress the need to remove the last vestiges of any feeling or attribution of guilt or blame from the process of ending one's marriage. "We may look forward, no doubt," writes Digby Anderson, Director of the Social Affairs Unit, "to tick-the-box divorce by return of post."

The gradual and conscious destruction of the public conscience in respect to divorce is certainly being paid for in misery. The direct sufferings of the children who are victims is vast. But quite apart from that, the vast increase in child abuse, in child delinquency and mental stress in children is indirectly related to the rising divorce rate. We see a rising number of one-parent families, fatherless children, and tension-wracked households.

That we have here a taste of hell on earth is indisputable, for we have a clear instance of what may properly be called the practice and the code of the Alternative society. When members of the Alternative society are faced with the dilemma—You may choose A or B, but if you choose B you and others will pay for it—they increasingly opt for the alternative B. B is more attractive immediately and superficially to many human beings. It always has been.

Stealing goods from the supermarket shelves is more immediately attractive than having to pay for them. The law comes to the aid of conscience, not only the law in the form of police and the courts, but also the law through the accepted code which will class the shoplifter as no longer respectable. Indulging in immorality with a new homosexual acquaintance is apparently more immediately attractive to some than refraining. The law no longer comes to the aid of the conscience, neither the law of the land nor in many circles the law in the form of the accepted code of social respectability. Sleeping with someone else's spouse may be more exciting than going home at the end of a party. The law has ceased to corroborate conscience. Indeed, both our public and private conscience has been eroded so that there is little or no individual resistance to sustain.

The result of the prevailing tendency to choose the wrong alternative is an epidemic of misery, cruelty, and disease. Much of the cruelty is caused unintentionally. For instance, we see the devastating effect upon children of parents' decisions to divorce made often in the name of what's best for everyone involved.

Ours is an age in which a genuine increase in compassion has produced works of public welfare on a scale that does credit to Western civilization. Yet, ironically enough, the social and moral changes in our society have caused a tragic increase in damage to our fellow human beings. The widespread collapse of the monogamous ethic has been accompanied by a rising tide of unspeakable brutality to children, of mindless vandalism by youth, of savage domestic violence, and agonizing mental breakdowns, of alcoholism and of drug addition, not to mention venereal diseases and AIDS in particular. Insofar as this represents the penalty for opting for the Alternative to the traditional codes of Christianity, it is a taste of hell on earth. Indeed, in this respect we are witnessing a wholesale incursion of the powers of hell on earth.

But there is a great difference between eternal punishment and suffering in this life. Eternal punishment is reserved for the guilty. Temporal suffering falls on the guilty and innocent alike. And if our society had in its bloodstream one fraction of an ounce of the compassion it so widely lays claim to, it would rise in rage against the pushers and practitioners of deadly moral decay. For it is the disintegration of the monogamous family which has brought misery to millions of innocent children—children whose innocence has been destroyed by the assault upon civilized morality.

It is reported that the Agricultural Commission of the European Common Market has decreed that in future all goats shall be classified as sheep. The decree makes a fit symbolic commentary on what western society has been doing in the area of morals through the decades of this century. By legislation and by education, by brainwashing the public with all the resources of the media, it has been systematically and ruthlessly obliterating the distinction between sheep and goats.

Suppose a great prophet had forecast fifty years ago where increasing permissiveness would lead us. And by great prophet I mean someone whose voice would have commanded public attention. Certainly voices have been raised, if weakly, in every decade of our century against the rising tide of permissiveness called the sexual revolution. What might have been the effect of a realistic prophetic forecast of possible moral dissolution comparable to George Orwell's forecast of possible political tyranny in *1984*?

People were duly alarmed when *1984* forecast what price would have to be paid by western nations if they failed in political vigilance. But what about the price that is now being paid for our lack of moral vigilance? It is true that in the years between the two World Wars Aldous Huxley in *Brave New World* foresaw a society populated by test-tube babies, the family destroyed, and sexuality reduced to a promiscuous pastime aided by oral contraception. There was a bleakness about that prospect drab enough to repel the young with their memories of love and romance.

But in Huxley's forecast there were no tortured babies with cigarette butts pressed against their chubby cheeks, their bodies a mass of bruises and burns. There were no teenagers cracking the skulls of old-age pensioners and making off with their purses and wallets. There was no virus running amok through sexual organs, condemning its victims to probable dementia and certain death, and threatening to decimate the human population by a physical disintegration as torturously slow as it was sure. In short, the easy self-indulgences of our new liberal age of permissiveness were foreseen by Huxley without their ugliest consequences.

We have seen how in private life and in the public domain the pattern of experience repeats itself: when the wrong choice is made, punishment and retribution invariably follow. It happens in the smallest and gravest of matters. You eat too many cream buns and your stomach is slightly uncomfortable. You throw your weight about too much at meetings of the social club, and resentful members vote you off the committee. You decide to risk leaving your car outside the bank, and you find yourself with a parking fine to pay. You rob a bank, and you are sent to prison. On the wider public scene, people opt for a more permissive society, and the scourge of AIDS descends upon them.

We might ask ourselves whether the Creator might not have devised a more reliably comfortable world for us to live in. Was it necessary that just when I am tempted to eat another piece of pie, a reminder of the onset of a stomachache should intervene and prove decisive? When I drive slowly along the city street late at night and an attractive woman stands in a pool of lamplight ready to be picked up, was it necessary that a painful reminder of the threat of venereal disease should make me desist at the crucial moment? Isn't there a bit too much of this business of having to pay for things built into our human pilgrimage?

Freedom and Penalty

The business of having to pay for things throws back momentousness onto the moment of choice. The penalty system built into our human situation charges the moment of choice with urgency. It enables us to exercise our freedom to some purpose. Indeed, the question whether or not to eat another piece of pie would not be worth weighing if there were no such thing as indigestion or some other penalty for overeating. If an act is in itself lacking in significant consequences, we shrug our shoulders and say, "It's neither here nor there."

We cannot get excited about choices where alternative consequences are indistinguishable. Freedom itself could surely not be meaningful in a world where human choices never resulted in regrets but always in satisfaction. It appears to be the penalty for making the wrong choice which gives the act of choosing its significance. In other words, that is the point of freedom.

Does it follow from this that life as a whole would lack significance and momentousness if the major choices people make could never result in a final penalty? We know that with cunning and luck many avoid penalties in this life. We cannot of course avoid all suffering by cunning, only by luck. For there is suffering that is not the consequence of any evident cause—like cancer or multiple sclerosis. But then these are not penalties since they are not based upon choices we have made—except where cancer is traceable to some known cause such as cigarette smoking. Thus, there is no connection with freedom when this type of suffering occurs.

But we are concerned with suffering brought upon oneself

by the self's own action. That is the nature of punishment. It is punishment that throws back urgency on the act of choice. Without it, the act of choice would be a matter only for shrugging the shoulders over. Freedom seems to be unthinkable without punishment. By this logic we are driven to the conclusion that if our lives could never in any circumstances end in punishment, then they would not deserve to be called truly free. A life which could never be followed by punishment would be morally trivialized and emptied of true freedom.

Consider some of the weightier matters in which your life has presented you with some choice. Shall I ask this woman to marry me? Shall I accept this man's offer of marriage? Shall we send this difficult child away to a special school? Shall I accept my son and daughter-in-law's suggestion that I go and live in their home? Shall I opt for immediate surgery or for some long-term alternative therapy? Shall we have a baby? Shall I take this post in a foreign land? Shall we stretch our resources to purchase that attractive house?

In all these cases the exercise of freedom is momentous because when the choice has been made the consequences will be good *or* bad. In other words, there will be a reward if it proves to be the right decision and a penalty or punishment if it proves to be the wrong one.

The penalty is not always paid by the chooser alone, of course. And the reward is not only or always enjoyed by the chooser alone. Some choices themselves have more significance for others than the choosers themselves. A surgeon ponders the problem, "Shall I amputate the leg of this eighty-six-year-old man? It would have to be done above the knee in this case. Even though it would immediately end his pain, there might well be a recurrence of the trouble. In any case, what sort of life is he going to enjoy, if that is the right word?" The major reward of the right choice will be reaped by the patient and the major penalty of the wrong choice will be paid by the patient. This is not to deny that the surgeon will be pleased if his choice proves a blessing to the man and saddened if it proves a bane.

In all these cases the act of choice takes its urgency and gravity from the fact that if the wrong choice is made there will be a price to be paid. The exercise of freedom thus takes its meaning from the possibility of subsequent punishment. This principle is built into the very fabric of our lives. It gives a weight to our vocations on this planet which they would otherwise lack. Remove all future consequence of reward or penalty from human decisions, and the questions "Shall I marry her?" and "Shall I amputate his leg?" are plainly on the same level as "Shall I wear my blue hat or my green one?" Life becomes trivial.

To speculate on the afterlife is an awesome matter. There is one hypothetical scenario, however, which is so offensive to the human reason and the human conscience as to merit being labelled obscene. Picture the hereafter. Some of those great saints we have known are gathered in a group. Some of the unworthiest people we have known are gathered in another group. Like has tended to drift to like after death. In the first group will be men and women who have devoted themselves to God's service in worship and good works with a zeal, self-discipline, and self-sacrifice which we admire from afar. Some of them forsook home comforts, gave up marriage and family life, turned their backs on lucrative careers, and spent themselves arduously for God and their fellow men.

In the second group are men and women who, in their various ways, served self—not in all cases crudely ammassing riches and luxuries, but in their various ways always trying to ensure that they got what they wanted out of life. Their prime motivation was always a self-centered one. Many of their acquaintances suffered as a result through crossing their paths and meeting envy, hatred, slander, mockery, and other injury. An objective judge with a bird's eye view of the human scene could point to hearts broken, lives wrecked, minds soiled, and homes broken as a consequence of the way this group of people lived.

Meanwhile, the same judge—surveying the human scene on

which the first group of people left their mark—can see souls grateful for their generosity, whole in mind and body because of their service, happy through having learned from their example. The first group of people are men and women who have left behind them on earth a trail of comfort and blessedness, while the second group have left behind them a trail of human misery.

Can we conceivably picture a hereafter in which the distinction between these groups becomes irrelevant? Can we picture an angelic company receiving the two groups of men and women and utterly discounting what made some lives heroic and some despicable? Are all human moral sensitivities to be finally laughed at by smiling angels as an uproarious joke? "These people thought it mattered! They actually thought it mattered, the business of being good or evil!"

If we are tempted to entertain the idea that all moral exercise of human freedom can be ground ultimately into the dust of meaninglessness, then we must know what we are about. It puts the death of the heroic martyrs on the same level as the suicide of a trapped tyrant. It puts Christ on the same level as Satan. It is the final apostasy.

THREE

The Nature of Hell

Good and Evil

Let us steal inside the walls of a fashionable private club. We peek into the writing room, with its elegant kneehole desks around the walls, laden with silver penholders and envelope racks. At the very moment of our entry, two men are sitting down against opposite walls of the room. By an odd coincidence they seem to be going through exactly identical procedures. Each one takes a piece of stationery from a drawer, an envelope from a rack, and a checkbook from his pocket. Each writes on the stationery, writes on a check, writes on the envelope, then rises with a smile of contentment on his face and goes off to put the letter in the club mailbox.

The two men and their acts are mirror images of each other. Yet if an angel were looking down on the scene he would have smiled on Mr. Smith's performance and frowned on Mr. Hall's. For Mr. Smith has just heard of the grave troubles of an old friend, stricken with cancer and undergoing major surgery while his wife is severely short of cash even to keep up mortgage payments on their home. Mr. Smith has written privately to his friend's banker, enclosing a check for one thousand dollars to be paid anonymously into his friend's checking account. Mr. Smith is not so wealthy that he can painlessly draw checks for one thousand dollars on his personal account, but he and his wife have agreed to call off a planned holiday in Greece in order to help an old friend.

Mr. Hall, alas, has been about no such charitable undertaking. Quite the reverse. When his aunt became insane he was put in charge of her affairs. He has acted honorably in this respect up till now, but some rash gambling on the stock exchange has lately put him into a financial jam. He has temporarily rescued himself from financial embarrassment by transferring a sum from his aunt's account to his own, and so today he was able to draw a check for one thousand dollars on his personal account to mollify a creditor who had gotten to the stage of sending threatening letters.

We said an angel looking down on the scene in the club would have smiled on the one man's act and frowned on the other's. But if, for purposes of argument, we were to indulge the fancy that there could be such a thing as a young angel inexperienced in human affairs under the direction of a wise old angel thoroughly experienced in human affairs, then clearly the young angel might be confused as to why he should smile on one act by one man as being good and frown on the seemingly identical act by another man as being evil.

When the words good and evil are used with moral force, they tend to call up vastly different pictures. Yet when our imaginary young angel is taken on his apprenticeship tour of the human scene, he has to be taught that there can be a strange ostensible identity between good and evil behavior. He is shown a promiscuous married man in the act of seducing his neighbor's daughter. Then he is shown a bridegroom and bride consummating their marriage in a hotel bedroom.

Angels have no sex, and when the young angel is told how wicked and ugly the first act is and how good and beautiful the second act is, he is naturally inclined to reply, "But these two couples are both doing the same thing!" Again, he catches sight in one place of a vicious murderer beginning to hack off the limbs of his victim to reduce the person to a dismembered torso. Then in another place, he witnesses a surgeon amputating the legs of a patient lying on a hospital operating table. He is puzzled and needs to be instructed why one act is viciously brutal and the other a work of mercy.

We have taken the liberty of imagining a degree of naivete which an angel, even if a young one, would surely not be guilty of. But it is with the worthy purpose of trying to penetrate to the essential difference between good and evil. Without understanding that difference, we can scarcely expect to conceive the nature of hell. There is nothing intrinsically evil about writing a check, or Mr. Smith would have done an evil thing in aiding his friend. There is nothing intrinsically evil about the sexual act, or the honeymoon couple would have been wicked to consummate their marriage. There is nothing intrinsically evil about taking a saw to a man's leg, or the surgeon would have been wicked to do what he did.

It is a good thing that a man has a brain. It is a good thing that he exercises it. It is a good thing when the exercise is directed towards a plan to build a new hospital. It is a bad thing when the exercise is directed towards a plan to rob a bank. It is a good thing that a man has a voice. It is a good thing that he exercises it to communicate with his fellows. It is a good thing when the communication enlightens the hearer, or when it expresses gratitude, appreciation, or love. It is a bad thing when the communication deceives or corrupts the hearer, or when it expresses resentment, mockery, or hatred. The can of meat on the supermarket shelf is a good thing. Your determination to take it home to feed the children is a good thing. Their enjoyment of it is a good thing. And the sustenance it gives them is a good thing.

Yet evil enters into the total otherwise wholesome sequence if you slip the can past the cash register without paying for it. When you come to think about it, the amount of good happening in the world at any one time is immeasurably vast and extensive compared to the amount of evil. Yet when you read that Mrs. Brown has been stealing meat from the supermarket, you shake your head gravely and you picture a whole sequence infected with evil from wickedly snatching the can of meat, slyly slipping it into a bag and concealing it from the clerk at the cash register, blandly passing it off on the family as an honest purchase, and involving them in the squalid business of eating stolen goods. What a trivial little act, that deception at the cash register, to spread its influence so widely.

Such is the permeative character of evil. Yet there could be no evil if there were not something good for the permeation to work upon. There could be no theft, no dishonesty, no deception by Mrs. Brown, were there no wholesome nutriment in the cans, no enjoyable family meal, no eager satisfying of healthy young appetites at home. To that extent evil is parasitic. It cannot stand on its own feet. It can only become effective by attaching itself to Mrs. Brown's otherwise virtuous activity in obtaining worthwhile food for healthy appetites.

Present evil with a virtuous activity and it can cling to it like a burr to a sweater and be carried where otherwise it would never go alone. For we have seen that even the sawing off of a person's leg is not of itself an evil act. It is done daily in the world's hospitals to restore otherwise doomed men and women to a tolerably healthy life. Evil insinuates itself into the process when it is done, not to cure a patient, but to destroy someone.

And we have seen that the sexual act is not of itself evil. On the contrary it is the divinely ordained means of bringing men and women together for the procreation of children and the continuance of the human race. Evil insinuates itself into the act when it is done, not out of love within the divinely ordained institution of marriage, but out of selfish lust, or the desire to corrupt, or the will to steal what belongs to another. Once more there is no substantial act or entity standing on its own which we can call evil. There is only a parasitic invader disseminating its virus through the frame of an otherwise wholesome act.

Now a reader may protest that the argument is being rigged, and may point to horrific acts of murder and obscene brutalities committed by the forces of police states and say, "There you have pure evil, undiluted." But such evil is purely destructive. And what is destructive has to have something to destroy. All destructive evil is parasitic in that it cannot exist in a vacuum.

By its very nature it has to fasten itself on something to destroy it. Even an SS officer wielding a whip could only function evilly because he had a healthy arm to misuse and the back of a worthy fellow human being to bring it down on. That's how *dependent* evil is upon good for its operation. Indeed, if the victim lashed by the SS man were not himself a good man but one who had done much evil, we should not consider his whipping quite as evil as the whipping of an innocent, unselfish, or saintly person. The more righteous, the more innocent, the better the victim of brutality, the more evil the act of brutality becomes. To that extent evil is dependent upon good. The better the thing evil latches on to, the more terribly evil can operate. If there is not a sign of goodness anywhere, evil can do nothing at all.

For this reason I have sometimes wondered whether the image of a Christian soldier fighting the forces of evil does not give a misleading picture by falsely dignifying evil, by giving it a status and an independence which it does not possess. "Onward, Christian soldiers, marching as to war" is rousing stuff, but it suggests preparation for a pitched battle. The cross of Jesus is held aloft and the Christian soldiers advance behind it. Shields are gripped and swords are raised to tackle a foe of substance on the field of battle. But evil does not have such independent substance. If the Christian host is marching forward and evil is assailing it, then it is more like a virus trying to spread its infection through the system of each soldier than an opponent casting down a gauntlet and challenging his foe to mortal combat.

If you have an electric kitchen range and an element burns out, you say, "The range is defective. It's not as good as it once was. Only three of its four elements work." Then, if a second element burns out, you say, "The kitchen range is quite defective. Only two of the four cooking elements work." Finally, if all four elements burn out, you say, "The top of the kitchen range is no use at all. It won't work." In fact, it has ceased to exist. By stages its defects have removed from the range the qualities that made it an effective means of cooking. A kitchen range top which you can no longer cook on is for all practical purposes non-existent.

Similarly, if you have a beautiful bowl into which you pour milk at breakfast for cereal, and it gets knocked around so that there is a crack running down one side, you find that you can no longer fill it as full as you did because the milk trickles out of the crack. "That bowl is defective," you say. You mean that for practical purposes it is less of a bowl than it was, since a bowl's function is to hold liquid and this one no longer holds the amount it was designed to hold. But if the bowl gets another knock and falls into pieces, it can no longer be used as a bowl at all. You describe it as a "broken bowl." But it is a bowl broken to such an extent that for practical purposes it is no longer a bowl at all.

Defects destroy material objects. The greater the defect is, the less the object can serve its purpose. All these examples illustrate the character of evil. Like any other defect, evil detracts from the reality of what it affects. Defects accumulate until the kitchen range top ceases to be a range top. Defects accumulate until the bowl ceases to be a bowl. And comparable defects may accumulate until a human being is hardly human any longer.

In the extreme case we speak as though that is what happens. It may be mental and physical defects and we say, "He has become little more than a vegetable." Or it may be moral defects and we say, "He has become little more than an animal." The logic is clear enough. A man's purpose here in the Christian view is to live a good life in the loving service of God and his fellow human beings. Insofar as he fails to do so he fails to be fully human. For his purpose in Christian eyes is as definite as the purpose of the kitchen range top or the milk bowl, and if he does not fulfill it he falls short of being fully human. Small wonder that we say "Be a man!" to some fellow when we want to urge him to pull himself together.

The Nature of Evil

Augustine records in his *Confessions* how, at a crucial stage in his conversion, he wrestled philosophically with the problem of evil. He had been a Manichee, that is to say he had come to believe that good and evil were at war in the universe, two mighty supernatural forces ranged against each other on something like an equal footing. He could not reconcile the notion of God's omnipotent goodness, as Creator of all things, with the presence of evil in the world. Then the crucial truth occurred to him that evil was not a substantial, positive force with its own grounding in supernatural reality, but a totally negative force only operative by eroding what is good, depleting it, and eventually destroying it.

This is in fact the only logical alternative to the Manichean view of a dualistic universe in which the power of evil challenges God on its own basis of authority and power. There is no room for such a rival basis of authority and power in a universe created by an almighty God who is all goodness. Any authority or power in the universe must be derivative from God—whether healthy or corrupt. There is no evil thing that is not a good thing corrupted. There is no evil being who is not a good being perverted.

The mysteries of the hereafter are not to be lightly peered into. It is only by exercise of the poetic imagination that heaven is pictured in the Bible, and it is only by the exercise of the poetic imagination that hell could be convincingly pictured. It so happens that an attempt was made by the great English poet John Milton in *Paradise Lost* to picture both heaven and hell. No one could have been more fitted to make the attempt. Heaven is all light and beauty and joy, all order and harmony, all love and courtesy. By contrast, hell negates all these qualities.

Milton takes great pains to represent evil as it should be represented. There is nothing in this hell which is not a perversion or distortion or negation of what there is in heaven. Everything that happens in hell is derivative by corruption and parody of what happens in heaven. For instance, there is a council in heaven where God sits surrounded by the angelic hosts enjoying the bliss of the beatific vision. The Son is enthroned on his right hand, "the radiance of his glory," as in Hebrews 1:3 (NIV). God's all-seeing eye detects what is happening in hell and what is to happen on his newly created earth, where Adam and Eve live in innocence and bliss.

He sees Satan's plan to bring about their transgression and fall. There is a good deal of theological argument about how the gift of freedom to humanity has made their fall possible and at the same time about how good they were created, how fully the fall will be their own responsibility. But the main gist of Milton's debate revolves around the question: how are we going to save them? The terrible cost of saving them through a sacrifice of love and justice is spelled out. We see the need for an atoning victim.

The argument is tight and subtle. Freely offered divine grace and mercy are available to penitent man, but man's sin destroys the relationship within which mercy could be sought and granted, the relationship of the creature to the Creator. To break creaturely obedience is to try to undermine the supremacy of heaven. It is an attempt to pose as God. It parallels Satan's own act of rebellion in being essentially *discreational*; that is to say, it reverses the pattern of things (the Creator-creature relationship) by which the Creator made the world and man within it.

Thus, improper self-assertion turns creation toward dis-creation or destruction. Willing self-sacrifice alone can turn the discreational back into its rightful creational grooves. As the creature usurped the Creator's authority and the human dislodged the divine, so the divine must put on creaturely humility and willingly assume the human. Which of the heavenly beings, God asks, has charity equal to the task?

Milton's argument is a packed and logical sequence in which the intellect operates with a delightfully coherent and rational force. At the conclusion of God's declaration, the Son offers himself as the atoning victim ready to assume humanity and accept man's punishment by substitution. The Son will conquer death by freely submitting himself to it as a being whose divine essence and character are alien to death's authority and uncontainable within its grasp.

There is no need to go further in analysis of some finely subtle passages in *Paradise Lost* in order to make the point desired. It is that in the packed theological argument there is an astonishing cohesion and symmetry with a sure intellectual and even aesthetic appeal. The poise and precision with which the reasoning moves, sequence by sequence, breathe verve and vitality in spite of the abstract nature of the thought. But when Milton paints the picture of hell it is to turn the tables on every quality enjoyed in heaven.

For hell too has its council. The fallen angels hold a debate under Satan's eye about what their future policy must be, heaven being for the moment lost to them. The debate parodies the debate in heaven. Where the heavenly argument revolved around the question: how can we save mankind? the hellish debate revolves around the question: how can we destroy mankind? As the heavenly debate leads to the Son's offer to go to earth to sacrifice himself for man's salvation, so the hellish debate leads to Satan's proposal to go to earth to bring about man's damnation. The Son is moved by love and mercy. Satan is moved by the desire to win kudos as the great adventurer who will stop at nothing.

Even more striking is the connection between heaven and hell in the respective character and quality of the debates. In heaven it is all tight logic and precise reasoning. In hell each of the devils who contributes to the debate indulges in the bogus tricks of persuasion which we have come to associate with politicians, journalists, and advertisers. High-sounding rhetoric, when examined, proves fallacious, illogical, even self-contradictory.

Any apparent appeal to intellect is specious. Emotive devices and absurd exaggerations are exploited to brainwash the listeners into agreement. Every trick in the armory of the deceptive propagandist is played in total scorn for overall consistency and coherence. By concealment of their real intentions and their true motives, speakers work upon their audience in order to glorify themselves and to forward their self-interest. There is not a disinterested word spoken. Everyone is using the resources of intellect and the resources of rhetoric to get an effect while putting rationality to sleep. Irony, sarcasm, mockery, vituperation, boasting, deception, mock humility—name a posture or a verbal device that offends against the canons of logic, reason, courtesy, honesty, and decency, and you will find it exploited in the debate between the devils in Milton's hell.

The message is clear. The attempt of the devils to be something, to do something, to say something is nothing but a perverse parody of what happens in heaven. As reason and logic are exercised in heaven, so in hell the powers of the intellect are perverted into an instrument for deceiving, showing off, and getting one's own way. Hell, after all, turns out to be nothing but a mock-up heaven run by self-seekers who have rejected the real thing. So quite apart from its horrendous physical environment whose topographical and climactic disorders are a negation of the light and beauty and peace of heaven, its horrendous psychological and mental disorders are a negation of the intellectual order and harmony obtaining in heaven, where clear minds play with subtle ideas in sheer rhythmic delight.

Nowhere is the doctrine that evil is a perversion of good more vividly set forth than in Milton's hell. Satan himself is a mock hero posturing in parody of heaven's King and the Son. There is even a hellish trinity in parody of the Holy Trinity in heaven. For when Satan first conceived the idea of disobedience and rebellion, Sin sprang to life from his head. Satan sees his own perfect image reflected in her. She is his perfect image as the Son is the perfect image of the Father. The Father's love of the Son is perverted into Satan's incestuous and self-centered lust for the one in whom he sees himself reflected.

On her he begets the monster Death. So Death proceeds in hell from the diabolical Father and his daughter as the Holy Ghost proceeds in heaven from the Father and the Son. In hell Death lusts incestuously after his mother Sin and begets on her a monstrous progeny.

The parodic trinity in hell is illuminating because it helps to illustrate not only the relationship between heaven and hell, but also the relationship between heaven and earth. For there is a human trinity as well as divine and diabolical trinities. Eve derives from Adam as the Son is begotten of the Father and Sin of Satan. Just as Sin's relationship to Satan in hell parodies the Son's relationship to the Father in heaven, so Eve's relationship to Adam in Paradise images the Son's relationship to the Father in heaven.

If hell is the parody of heaven, Paradise is the image of heaven. There is an image in man and woman of the divine consubstantiality of Father and Son. Fatherhood and Sonship in unity express the glory of Godhead. Manhood and womanhood in unity express the glory of humanity. If there is a relationship of authority and obedience between man and woman, it is no more remarkable than that between Father and Son. The equality of Father and Son is not impaired by this relationship. Nor is the equality of man and woman.

It is important to note that the pattern of obedience relating God to man and man to woman (and the Father to the Son) is the reverse of that initial disobedience, angelic and human, by which all harmonious relationships have been destroyed. The offspring of Adam and Eve will of course proceed from the human father and her in whom he delights as the Holy Spirit proceeds from the Father and the Son in whom he delights.

This little summary of some of Milton's poetic correspondences is made in order to bring out the relationship between heaven, earth, and hell. As Adam and Eve and their coming family are put on earth to image the life of the divine

Trinity in heaven, so Satan and his progeny represent a defiant parody of that life in hell. And as the Garden of Eden in which Adam and Eve are placed mirrors in all its delights and beauties the heaven where God himself dwells; so hell, whither the fallen angels are directed, represents a negation of all joy, beauty, harmony, and peace.

We must remember, however, that Milton's hell is a pre-human hell. We look into it and get our fullest picture of it before ever man has fallen. By the very character of the story he was telling, Milton could not focus—as Dante did—on a hell where once-living human beings are suffering all kinds of torments for their misdeeds on earth. This limitation compelled Milton to concentrate on the very concept of hell itself as the home of evil and the environment of evil, and on Satan and the fallen angels as the source of all evil—its ultimate originators and its wholehearted practitioners.

Punishment and Destruction

In the King James Version of the Bible the word "hell" is used in translating two separate Hebrew words, *Sheol* and *Gehenna*. *Sheol* means "the Underworld" and is the equivalent of the Greek word *Hades*, which is frequently used in modern translations of the Bible. It is the dwelling place of departed spirits in a somewhat nebulously conceived future existence. Sometimes *Sheol* is translated as "hell," sometimes as "grave," sometimes as "pit." The second Hebrew word translated as "hell" is *Gehenna*. Gehenna was originally the valley of Hinnom southwest of Jerusalem. Its associations were with the worship of idols and with human sacrifice. We are told how the righteous King Josiah polluted it: "And he defiled Topheth, which is in the valley of the children of Hinnom, that no man might make his son or his daughter to pass through fire to Molech" (2 Kgs 23:10).

The place began to be used as a rubbish heap and it has been said that fires were kept burning there to destroy the refuse.

Thus the name Gehenna was used of the dwelling place of the devil and his angels, a place of everlasting fire to which the condemned spirits of human beings were consigned. It is to *Gehenna* that our Lord condemns the wicked in Matthew 5:22 ("Whosoever shall say, Thou fool, shall be in danger of hell fire") and in Matthew 5:30 ("And if thy right hand offend thee, cut it off, and cast it from thee; for it is profitable for thee that one of thy members should perish, and not that thy whole body should be cast into hell").

The distinction between *Sheol* and *Hades* on the one hand, and *Gehenna* on the other hand is not one which need trouble a modern reader. For though, for instance, it is the word *Sheol* which is used by our Lord in describing where the rich man Dives is confined ("And in hell he lift up his eyes, being in torments, and seeth Abraham afar off, and Lazarus in his bosom," Lk 16:23), the fact that Dives is "in torments" is crucial to the story. That is why Dives seeks to have the tip of his tongue cooled by water—"for I am tormented in this flame," he tells Abraham (Lk 16:24).

Moreover, the impassable gulf fixed between Dives in his place of torment and Lazarus in his place of blessed repose is precisely what separates hell from heaven. It is plain that the accepted Christian tradition has done no violence to biblical teaching in this respect. Nor did Milton do any violence to biblical teaching in focusing on the hell to which fallen man will be in danger of condemnation as the pre-human dwelling place of the fallen angels. For in our Lord's account of the last judgment in which the sheep on the right hand are separated from the goats on the left hand, it is precisely to this dwelling place of the devils that the wicked are consigned: "Then shall he say also unto them on the left hand, Depart from me, ye cursed, into everlasting fire, prepared for the devil and his angels" (Mt 25:41). In this crucial vision of judgment, the condemnation of souls to eternal torment is not complicated by the use of either term *Sheol* or *Gehenna*, but the meaning is unmistakable.

The New Testament will not allow us to wriggle out of confrontation with the fact that the wicked will pay a penalty. In the Epistle to the Romans, the apostle Paul foresees "the day of wrath and revelation of the righteous judgment of God" (Rom 2:5), the day when God "will render to every man according to his deeds: To them who by patient continuance in well doing seek for glory and honor and immortality, eternal life: But unto them that are contentious, and do not obey the truth, but obey unrighteousness, indignation and wrath, Tribulation and anguish, upon every soul of man that doeth evil" (Rom 2:5-9). The righteous are promised "glory, honor, and peace" (Rom 2:10), but the unrighteous shall perish (Rom 2:12).

The apostle Paul returns to the subject of judgment at the beginning of the Second Epistle to the Thessalonians. He praises the members of the Thessalonian church for showing great endurance and faith in the tribulations and persecutions they have been subjected to. They are promised their reward when the Lord Jesus comes again from heaven with his angels around him. Christ will be seen in "flaming fire taking vengeance on them that know not God, and that obey not the gospel of our Lord Jesus Christ: Who shall be punished with everlasting destruction from the presence of the Lord, and from the glory of his power" (2 Thes 1:8-9).

This is a significant statement, for it expands the various scriptural references to the fate of perishing, or being destroyed, which awaits lost souls. The apostle John's celebrated declaration "God so loved the world, that he gave his only begotten Son, that whosoever believeth in him should not perish, but have everlasting life" (Jn 3:16) implies that the alternative to achieving eternal life is to *perish*. The constant repetition in the New Testament of the promise of everlasting life seems to suggest death rather than everlasting torment as its counterpart.

Indeed, we might well think that an emphasis upon salvation as everlasting joy would be more appropriate if its counterpart were everlasting torment. But the apostle Paul's words to the Thessalonians, quoted above, "everlasting destruction from the presence of the Lord," link the notion of destruction with deprivation of God's presence and the glory of his power. It is appropriate therefore that modern translators of the Bible stress this aspect of the apostle's message. J.B. Phillips writes of those who have "refused to know God or to obey the gospel of our Lord Jesus" that "their punishment will be eternal exclusion from the radiance of the face of the Lord, and the glorious majesty of his power." It will mean being "cut off from the presence of the Lord and the splendour of his might," as the New English Bible puts it.

Readers who have followed our argument so far will recall that all evil is deficiency of good and corruption of good, and that corruption of good is deprivation of good—for only what is good can stand on its own. So evil has whatever existence it has only by feeding on the good and perverting it. Therefore, the ultimate cost of denying the good and rejecting the good is self-destruction.

All that is good in the world is derivative from God's creative work. All that is evil in the world represents a depletion or distortion of that creative work, a movement towards *dis-creation* or *destruction*. Philosophically speaking, the ultimate end to which discreation or destruction moves, to which depletion or deprivation moves, is nothingness or annihilation. It is not therefore surprising to find the vocabulary of death, destruction, and perishing mixed up with the vocabulary of torment, anguish, "weeping and wailing and gnashing of teeth" in New Testament forecasts of the fate of the damned.

We human beings cannot combine the notion of endless torment with the notion of death or destruction. What is endless must go on and on indefinitely. On the other hand, total destruction must involve an abolition of consciousness which is final. It could be argued that at the point where the human mind runs up against a brick wall in its exploration of the hereafter it must accept the mystery. No doubt many readers will share my own conviction that a God of love will tell you what you need to know. If there are things he does not reveal to his children in this life, that is because we would be no better off if he had made them plain. The warnings about the fate of the damned are clear enough.

The seemingly irreconcilable destinies of endless torment and total destruction can be said to be reconciled only insofar as the apostle Paul reconciled them in his reference to destruction as deprivation of God's presence. The tendency among theologians today is rightly to lay emphasis on this aspect of damnation. Human beings have free will. If they persistently choose to exercise it in the service of self rather than in obedience to God, the rejection of God must logically become a final and irretrievable separation of the self from God. This means separation from the source and sustainer of all life and goodness. It clearly involves a total deprivation of happiness and peace.

In Marlowe's play, *Dr. Faustus,* Faustus sells his soul to the Devil in exchange for restoration to youth. The devil Mephistopheles is put at his service and Faustus questions him about himself and his lot. Mephistopheles confesses that he is one of those unhappy spirits who conspired against God with Lucifer, fell with him, and are eternally damned with him. Then where are you damned? Faustus asks. "In hell," Mephistopheles answers. Then what are you doing here, out of hell? Faustus asks, and Mephistopheles gives his famous reply:

> Why this is hell, nor am I out of it.
> Thinkest thou that I, who saw the face of God,
> And tasted the eternal joys of heaven,
> Am not tormented with ten thousand hells
> In being deprived of everlasting bliss?

This is a perceptive attempt to express the torment of hell in terms of the deprivation of the eternal joys of heaven. Such a version of hellish torment depends, of course, on continuing consciousness, on an existence which stops short of annihilation.

Milton touches briefly on the problem in the council held by the devils in hell. The debate revolves around the question what to do next, in particular whether there can be any further direct assault on the forces of God which have defeated them and cast them into hell. Or should they seek some indirect means of revenge on God such as the plan for an assualt on his favored creatures on earth? On the question of whether to attempt another head-on clash with the heavenly hosts, the devils divide into hawks and doves.

Moloch, the representative of bloodthirsty cruelty, naturally leads the hawks. He argues for a renewed assault on heaven. His case is that the devils have nothing to lose because—if God in anger struck any further blows at them—they would expire. They have already reached the nadir of existence, the bottom rung on the ladder of being. Any further measure of destruction would annihilate them, and to be annihilated would be preferable to continuing existence on their present level of misery.

It falls to the leader of the doves to reply to this argument. Belial, the representative of the softer vices, lust and ease, ridicules Moloch's logic. In the first place continued existence, however painful, is always preferable to annihilation. In the second place, if annihilation *were* preferable to continued existence—as Moloch thinks—then clearly it would be the last thing God would grant them. It is absurd to imagine that in a fit of temper God is going to reward a further assault upon heaven by doing them the favor of giving them exactly what they want.

The purpose of this further reference to Milton is to indicate that the seeming irreconcilability of the notion of everlasting punishment with the threat of total annihilation has been a problem for centuries. As we have seen, the problem is already latent in the New Testament in the competing threats of everlasting fire on the one hand and death or destruction on the other hand.

The Lot of the Damned

With the help of Milton we have taken a look into the minds of devils in hell. Is there any way of conceiving what might happen in the minds of human beings condemned to hell? The reader might suggest that there is a question which ought to be asked by the writer before asking that one: namely, have I any right to try to picture more exactly what God has left shrouded in mystery?

It is a troublesome question, for there is no doubt that excessive curiosity about the future life leads people into murky and dangerous waters, as the activities of spiritualists reveal. Yet there is a general and a special reason for making the effort here to portray imaginatively what must always remain hidden from men and women on this earth. The general reason is that we live in an age where, even in Christian circles, damnation and hell are no longer treated as seriously as they should be. The special reason, of course, is that if a man is asked to write a book about heaven and hell, he must not try to evade the most worrying issues by concentrating solely on heaven.

In point of fact, as a writer, I have no personal inclination to write about the afterlife. I am just seventy years old myself, and I feel that I shall know more about it soon enough. Better to make the most of whatever years remain with as little thought as possible of what comes next. It is tempting to make excuses for cutting down on hell in any study of the afterlife. Indeed, there is plainly something rather morbid about painting future torment in lurid terms. We react against it because it substitutes fear for love as a prime basis for Christian conviction. It endeavors to frighten people into faith, and that was not our Lord's way.

There is a celebrated section in James Joyce's autobiographical novel, *A Portrait of the Artist as a Young Man,* in which the young schoolboy, Stephen, attends a school retreat directed by an earnest Jesuit priest. Stephen has fallen into grave sin after being accosted one night in a Dublin street by a prostitute. A thoughtful boy with a deeply idealistic streak, he is deeply moved to a sense of his own wickedness by the retreat sermons delivered by Fr. Arnall.

But Joyce's account of the experience is a cunning mixture of gravity and humor. Fr. Arnall announces that his retreat sermons are to be on the Four Last Things: death, judgment, hell, and heaven. But when he comes to hell, his enthusiasm for the topic runs away with him. The torments of the damned and the ingenious tortures designed for them are painted in lurid colors. Fr. Arnall is plainly obsessed, and the retreatants never get a glimpse of heaven. When the time comes for the final sermon Fr. Arnall proves incapable of dropping his favorite subject and indulges instead in a further orgy of rhetoric on the pains of hell.

If some Jesuit priests in nineteenth century Dublin might have been inclined to lay on hellfire sermons a little too eagerly and frequently, there could be no question of the subject being over-exploited in the twentieth century Anglo-Saxon world. We are a long way today from indulging in a dangerously obsessive preoccupation with hell and damnation. The writer cannot today excuse himself from tackling the subject because other people are overdoing it.

What Joyce was attacking was a way of portraying hell's physical torments so crudely as to reduce them to unintentional burlesque. The damned are imprisoned within walls four thousand miles thick, their bodies heaped together in such a tangle that one cannot move an arm in order to remove from the eye a worm that gnaws at it. The horror of the prison is increased by the stench, as all the world's filth and offal and scum runs into it as into a sewer. Add to this the choking fumes of the fire that consumes decomposed carcasses and the reeking stink of yet unburied rotting bodies and you get an idea of hell's atmospheric conditions.

In reacting against this absurd and unhealthy way of picturing hell's torments, we run the risk of going to the other extreme and of so spiritualizing hell that it loses its terrors. We talk of the supreme torment of hell as being the deprivation of heaven's glory. Yet in the back of our minds, there is a voice that whispers consolingly that the deprivation of heavenly glory may not sound like an eternal Christmas party, but it sounds a good deal more comfortable than earthly servitude in prison or lung cancer.

And yet in an age in which mental sickness is so prevalent as it is today, it should not be difficult to conceive of interior states of torment to which earthly burns and stabs, earthly writhing and choking and smells contribute nothing. There is an important distinction here between feasible ways of conceiving heaven and hell respectively. It can surely not be inappropriate to bring to mind earth's physical delights in picturing heaven—balmy air, the scent of flowers, the sight of meadows under a blue sky, the touch of loved hands. There seems to be here an appropriate ladder of sensitivity to climb in conceiving the state of the blessed. In any case, we have biblical justification for bringing the poetic imagination to bear on what pleases the eye and the ear and the nose in picturing God in glory. But conversely to picture hell initially in terms of arthritis or toothache, asthma or migraine, would surely be too patently crude.

Any mental punishment must involve some recapitulation of the past. If you feel guilty because you have lost your temper and caused pain to someone, the guilt involves reliving the occasion. You wish things had happened otherwise. You were blinded at the moment of anger to certain aspects of the situation which are now made clear to you. The pain innocently suffered by the recipient of your anger is present to your mind as it was not present when you lost your temper. In other words, you relive the experience with a fuller and clearer realization of what happened. But guilt realized and its cause relived in such a case presumably involves penitence, and there is no penitence as such in hell. What then is the character of impenitent regret proper to hell?

A case has recently been reported in the British press in which a doctor—let us call him Doctor X—was found guilty of murder and attempted murder. Dr. X was beginning to tire of his first wife—whom we will call Alice—when a woman doctor—whom we will call Jean—joined his medical team. Jean, separated from her husband, was a highly attractive woman some years younger than Dr. X, and he quickly fell in love with her. But Jean resisted his sexual advances, saying that she would respond to such advances only if he divorced his wife Alice. Dr. X took his wife Alice on a holiday to Spain. He gave her an injection which killed her and then persuaded the local doctor that she had died of a heart attack.

Alice was buried in Spain. Dr. X came back to England and claimed Jean as his mistress, then as his wife. Setting up a new home with her was financed on the proceeds of his late wife's life insurance. It was not long before Dr. X frightened his new wife by confiding in her that he had sacrificed Alice out of love for her. He was a socially ambitious man, anxious to rise in fashionable society, and he insured his new wife's life for a vast sum.

One day he planned the perfect murder. He gave Jean an injection which put her out. He drove her far away from home. He parked his car in a remote spot and hid her body in the undergrowth. He slit her throat with skill enough, he thought, to ensure that her death would follow after a delay of some time, during which he could return to his home area and be seen in his old haunts. Jean would appear to have been abducted and murdered.

Then things began to go wrong. There was a heavy frost which dried up the flow of blood from Jean's throat. By a remarkable fluke a naturalist came along examining the undergrowth in the business of tracking badgers. He found Jean and called the police. Jean was taken to a hospital and after intensive care began to recover. She had the secret of the first wife's murder as well as the knowledge of the attempt to kill her. When she told her story to the police, Alice's body was exhumed in Spain. A post-mortem examination of the body revealed morphine injection as the cause of death.

With a sentence of life imprisonment, Dr. X will have plenty of time to reflect on what he has brought upon himself. We need not picture him condemned to hell in order to speculate on the way his evil deeds will recoil upon him. He will relive a series of experiences in great torment of mind. Initially, no doubt, the torment will consist in the knowledge that with a bit more luck and a bit more cunning, he might have got away with it. Certainly it was most unfortunate for him that a heavy frost put a stop to the ebbing away of Jean's life as the blood slowly flowed from her neck. Certainly it was doubly unfortunate that a naturalist should have chosen to pursue his unusual hobby over precisely the few square feet where Jean's body lay.

Fool that he was, anyway, he should have finished off Jean decisively. That rather vain additional touch of professionalism in devising a lingering death had done him in. He had tried to be a shade too clever, too subtle. Then what about that absurdly rash revelation to Jean of what he had done to Alice? Surely the memory of this will make him kick himself.

Indeed, the major misfortunes and the major blunders are so obvious that Dr. X will scarcely trouble to reflect on the lack of wisdom in over-insuring a wife's life if you intend to do away with her. Then what about that buried wife in Spain—so easily exhumed? If you are going to pass off a murdered wife's corpse as a victim of a heart attack, would it not be better to transport the whole operation to some area where the telltale body could be cremated? And lastly, granted that all this ill luck had happened and all these blunders been made, would not a cautious man have disappeared into a foreign country before ever the police came knocking at the door?

I am trying to show how reliving the past can be a harrowing experience *even though no sense of guilt impinges*, even though the reliving of it sheds no healthy moral light on the individual's role. We must think better of Dr. X than to imagine that when he relives the past he will regret only the mistakes he made and the bad luck he suffered, all of which led to his unmasking and his arrest. We must think better of him than to imagine that he clenches his fists and says, "If only Jean had died! If only I'd finished her off! If only Alice's body had been cremated! If only I'd never breathed a word about Alice to Jean!"

We must think better of Dr. X than to attribute to him years of tormenting himself only with such amoral self-recriminations. But his case has been presented because we are trying to get some idea of the kind of reliving of evil which the damned must experience. It is a reliving which evades that sense of guilt which leads to true penitence.

Impenitence

In taking a case so sensational as Dr. X's we run a grave risk. Nothing is easier or more dangerous than to start picturing hell as primarily inhabited by notorious criminals. It may well be the case that Dr. X will gradually realize the full enormity of what he has done, will go through the anguish of genuine contrition, will turn to God and beg penitently for forgiveness. Indeed, it may well be that it is precisely such notorious acts of evil, with the appalling earthly penalties they bring, which are most likely to lead to thorough self-examination, to penitence, and to a plea for mercy. If it is right to try to picture human inhabitants of hell, it must surely be appropriate to turn our minds to less spectacular careers than that of a Dr. X, and at the same time to take a penetrating look into our own hearts.

Now here the writer faces a difficulty. He wants to illustrate his point by citing cases of unspectacular wickedness which is carried impenitently to the grave. So he begins to rack his brains, trying to recall some of the most unpleasantly self-centered people he has ever met, whose careers might be used to illustrate his point. Then he checks himself. Can it be right to bring to mind the failings of dislikable people for the purpose of populating even an imaginary hell?

Would not that process on the writer's part—that analysis and condemnation of other people's apparent failings—be precisely the kind of activity likely to make the writer himself a fit candidate for damnation? At one point in considering the writing of this book I was inclined to say to myself, "It's surely rather presumptuous to pretend you're fit to write about heaven, but there can't be any presumption in claiming to be knowledgeable about hell." But now I suggest that I got things the wrong way around.

After all, in order to picture heaven you don't have to pass judgment of any kind on anyone. All you have to do is to recall all the most saintly and joyful Christians you have known, and picture them getting their reward. But in order to picture hell, you've got to start recording and annotating all the nastiness you have observed in other people, emphasizing every defect, and then making a great conglomerate of this keenly observed human wickedness and saying, "There you are. That's what the damned are like!" Can writing a theological book possibly involve one in that kind of exercise?

There is one sure test to apply to a task of this kind. Can I ask God's blessing on it? Can I pray for the guidance of the Holy Spirit? It would be fair enough to call for divine inspiration for the task of picturing heaven. "O God, grant me vision and understanding and purity of heart so that what I write may not be utterly unworthy of the subject. Help me to bring to mind the thought and speech, the habits and acts of saintly men and women who have best revealed to me what people you choose for eternal blessedness." That is fair enough.

But how do I beg inspiration for the task of describing hell? "O God, grant me an insight into the ultimate depths of human wickedness, degeneration, and impenitence. Help me to recall in detail the thought and speech, the habits and acts of sinful and depraved men and women who have most surely revealed to me what kind of people you consign to damnation." It won't do. The prayer is itself an application for a one-way ticket to hell.

If we turn our lens on the sins of the impenitent, we must try not to personalize the sinners. But for every Dr. X who may be tempted to see his past career in terms of failures, mischances, and mistakes rather than in terms of wickedness, there must be many, many a Mr. Y whose moral record of impenitence does not look very different in the eyes of heaven, though he has never crossed swords with the law. The man whose life has been only a long career in search of self-satisfaction even at the most modest level of social achievement does not differ in essential motivation from Dr. X—however much he may differ in respect for the law and in cautious avoidance of risk.

Whenever a man is surrounded by people from whom he seeks admiration and subservience rather than an opportunity to help and to serve, the pattern of God's purpose is turned from creation to destruction. Wherever a man demands satisfaction of his vanity and open recognition of his talents rather than an opportunity to love and to serve, the divine purpose is subverted. A lifetime of supposed public service in bureaucracy, in government, in education, even in the church may be subtly adjusted at all points to the end of self-glorification.

The peaks of life may be for such a man the applause at the end of his speeches, the lavish votes of thanks proposed by those who play up to his weaknesses, the recognition he achieves by promotion or public honor, the appearance of his name and photograph in the newspaper, the precious minutes of exposure he attains on television. These may represent the nourishment on which his ego feeds.

At the end of it all, it is easy to imagine a reliving of the past in which the light of truth dawns, the thread of self-centeredness running through his career is made plain to him. He rejects the corruption, becomes truly contrite, and begs for mercy. But, as with Dr. X, it is also possible to imagine a re-living of the past into which guilt never intrudes, but only intensified anger and frustration at the failure to achieve public acclamation on a scale which his status denied him.

"If only I had flattered G, who later became chairman of the appointments committee, I might have got the promotion which would have taken me to the top. If only I had not jockeyed W off the governing body, he would never have organized that little cabal against me which damaged me with the powers-that-be. If only I had skipped through M's books and pretended to appreciate them, I might have picked up the hint that it was fashionable to play up to the conservationists a bit. She would have got me into that flashy circle which really dominated the cultural life of the town."

There is no need to leave one's path through life littered with corpses in order to equip oneself for immersion in the mental morass of "if onlys." There is no need to have a prison sentence to regret in order to be stimulated to a tormenting sequence of self-recrimination about chances missed which, if taken, might have led to the achievement of one's obsessive selfish desires.

It is only necessary to picture re-living devoid of penitence to guess what the human lot in hell must be like.

FOUR

The End of the World

The Second Coming

Christian teaching looks forward to a life after death which will separate the saved from the lost. In the New Testament the act of final divine judgment on the human race is associated with the return of Christ to the world. At the climax of his trial before the high priest, Jesus forecasts this return with solemnity and dignity. The forecast rebuts the high priest's challenge with a supernatural confidence.

If Jesus were not indeed the Son of God, such confidence would represent an insane fanaticism. For the high priest had been driven to exasperation by our Lord's silence in the face of the accusations brought against him:

> Again the high priest asked him, and said unto him, Art thou the Christ, the Son of the Blessed? And Jesus said, I am: and ye shall see the Son of man sitting on the right hand of power, and coming in the clouds of heaven. (Mk 14:61-62)

In ordinary human criminal cases we attach a special significance to the words of a man on trial for his life. The murderer, about to be condemned to death, was always given a chance to make a last statement before the black cap was donned and judgment pronounced. Of all Christ's statements, a special weight must surely attach to what he says when trapped and challenged in open court.

77

And what does Christ choose to say? Not that he has brought a new ethos of love to replace the old Jewish legalities, not that judges ought to exercise mercy, and not that in any case he has done nothing to merit the death penalty. Instead, he announces that the time will come when the tables will be turned. The man now in the dock before the established religious authorities of Jerusalem, the prisoner about to be condemned to death, will return in power and glory. It will then be impossible to withhold recognition of his divine authority.

The forecast of the Second Coming is spelled out in detail by our Lord to his disciples in the Gospel according to Matthew (Mt 24:4-44). This prophecy provides a healthy antidote to sentimentalizing the teaching of Christ. Christ foresees all manner of trials and tribulations for his followers. The last thing that could be read into this formal declaration of what the future holds is any notion of gradual progress by the human race towards peace and plenty, harmony and justice on earth. There is even a sentence which suggests that the end is not far off: "Verily I say unto you, This generation shall not pass, till all these things be fulfilled" (Mt 24:34).

But the events foretold in the prophecy are far too vast to be contained within the span of any human lifetime. There will be "wars and rumors of wars," and "nation shall rise against nation"; there will be "famines and pestilences," and Christ's followers will be "hated of all nations." Moreover, "this gospel of the kingdom shall be preached in all the world for a witness unto all nations," though false Christs and false prophets and bogus wonder-workers will arise to deceive men and women with delusive claims.

At the end of the long tale of tribulations, "such as was not since the beginning of the world to this time" (24:21), there will be great disturbances in the skies:

And then shall appear the sign of the Son of man in heaven: and then shall all the tribes of the earth mourn, and they shall see the Son of man coming in the clouds of heaven with power and great glory. And he shall send his angels with a great sound of a trumpet, and they shall gather together his elect from the four winds, from one end of heaven to the other. (Mt 24:30-31)

Any modern reader weighing these momentous words with the benefit of hindsight is bound to recognize the sweeping prophecy as one in which Christ casts his eyes over the future centuries.

Two urgent notes are sounded by Christ. One is that no man knows the day or the hour of the Second Coming. Only God the Father in heaven knows that. The second emphasis is that men and women must live in readiness, "Watch therefore: for ye know not what hour your Lord doth come" (Mt 24:42). The element of surprise is crucial. Men and women, by and large, will be taken off their guard.

It will be just as it was in the days of Noah. People were eating and drinking as usual, marrying just as though there were a future life to enjoy on earth. Then the flood came and submerged them all. Such thoughtlessness is unwise. If a householder knew that a cat burglar was going to climb through the bedroom window at three in the morning, he would make sure there was someone there to meet him. Yet our Lord will come with a far more terrifying and awesome threat to a man's complacency and contentment than any burglar, who can after all only remove a few worldly valuables. The warning is pressed home. The human race must be ever on the watch for the winding-up of the terrestrial experiment, the ringing down of the final curtain on the human drama. The parable of the wise and foolish virgins presses home the same message of our need for constant readiness.

In view of Christ's emphasis on the need for constant watchfulness for the Second Coming, it is not surprising that early disciples tended to look for it in their own lifetime. Indeed, we cannot but recognize the logic of the fact that our

Lord's words included a remark which encouraged this interpretation.

God plainly intended that all men and women in all times should be strengthened in obedience by the thought that Christ might come again at any moment. He could scarcely therefore have allowed his Son to release his contemporaries from any worries on that score by assuring them that he was talking about a remote future. They were not to be encouraged in the notion that they, at any rate, could rest secure in the knowledge that he would not return in their lifetime. Their job was to be ready.

From the apostle John we learn that "the Father judgeth no man, but hath committed all judgment unto the Son" (Jn 5:22). There is nothing to be surprised at in this. Christ is given authority to execute judgment on mankind precisely "because he is the Son of man" (Jn 5:27). The time will come when "all that are in the graves shall hear his voice, And shall come forth; they that have done good, unto the resurrection of life; and they that have done evil, unto the resurrection of damnation" (Jn 5:28-29).

The apostle Paul fills out the picture, telling how the Lord himself will descend from heaven to angelic acclamation:

> . . . and the dead in Christ shall rise first: Then we which are alive and remain [of which Paul assumes he will be one] shall be caught up together with them in the clouds, to meet the Lord in the air. (1 Thes 4:16-17)

At the same time vengeance will be taken on those who "know not God, and that obey not the gospel of our Lord Jesus Christ." They will be punished with "everlasting destruction from the presence of the Lord, and from the glory of his power" (2 Thes 1:9).

Belief in the Second Coming of Christ and the general judgment of mankind has been constant and emphatic in mainstream Christianity. But about the timing of Christ's

return and its effect on world history there has been considerable divergence of views even among Christians who
would fiercely claim to be orthodox. There is a memorable
passage in the Book of Revelation, where John sees an angel
coming down from heaven with the key of hell and a great
chain in his hand:

> And he laid hold on the dragon, that old serpent, which is
> the Devil, and Satan, and bound him a thousand years, And
> cast him into the bottomless pit, and shut him up, and set a
> seal upon him, that he should deceive the nations no more,
> till the thousand years should be fulfilled. (Rv 20:2 3)

This happy conception of a thousand-year period during
which the devil would be forcibly restrained from deceiving
men and women encouraged the notion of a future millen-
nium, that is a thousand years during which the rule of Christ
would be established on earth. During that age men and
women would live through a golden time of peace and joy
before being taken up with Christ into heaven. Belief in this
doctrine is known as millenarianism.

Literal interpretation of certain Old Testament texts can be
used to corroborate this view, notably Isaiah's prophetic vision
of the coming of Christ as the "rod out of the stem of Jesse" (Is
11:1). He will bring his righteousness to bear upon the poor
and meek, will slay the wicked, will restore Israel, and establish
a regime in which "the wolf shall dwell with the lamb, and the
leopard shall lie down with the kid; and the calf and the young
lion and the fatling together; and a little child shall lead them"
(Is 11:6). It is an idyllic picture of tranquillity and harmony
possessing God's earth: "They shall not hurt nor destroy in all
my holy mountain: for the earth shall be full of the knowledge
of the LORD, as the waters cover the sea" (Is 11:9).

Millenarianism has its roots too in pre-Christian Jewish
apocalyptic writings. Its history in the Christian church has
been controversial. It has been argued that New Testament

support for millenarian views is slight and—such as it is—textually ambiguous. Nevertheless, those many evangelicals who hold millenarian beliefs do so with an attachment which is all of a piece with their commitment to basic Christian doctrines such as the divinity of Christ and the virgin birth, doctrines that provide essential criteria for orthodoxy.

Millenarian Christians do not, however, present a united front. The Book of Revelation is a highly poetic text, heavily charged with metaphor. Interpreters who bring a stubborn literalism to bear upon its highly resonant prophetic visions tend to reach a variety of conclusions. The result is that competing schools of thought among millenarianists themselves present a diversity of scenarios for the winding up of human history.

It is not the business of this book to make great play over doctrinal issues about which earnestly committed Christians disagree. It is fair to say, however, that teaching about the Second Coming has been a focus for a great deal of sectarian theorizing by bodies on the periphery of the historic Christian tradition. In view of our Lord's clear statement that only the Father in heaven could know the day and the hour of the Second Coming, it is surprising how often the curiosity of some Christian denominations has focused on what must remain an insoluble mystery.

Some Christian churches have tried to turn the Second Coming and its effect on the human race into a clearly predictable program in which believers are granted an enviably happy role to play. Our Lord's emphasis was rather on the need for increasing watchfulness against an event which cannot be anticipated. When it does come, it will strike the whole human race with awe.

There was an occasion when a number of Sadducees tried to ridicule belief in the resurrection of the dead by presenting to our Lord the story of a woman who married one of seven brothers, was repeatedly widowed, and successively married each of the seven in turn. Whose wife will she be in the resurrection? they asked. Our Lord then spoke about the resurrection life as though it were the most natural thing in the world for him to define. There is no marrying in heaven, he explained. And not only is there no marriage for men and women in heaven, there is no death either. "Neither can they die any more: for they are equal unto the angels" (Lk 20:36). The resurrection of the dead, then, is not a crude resumption of earthly bodies with unchanged earthly appetites and limitations.

In the celebrated fifteenth chapter of the First Epistle to the Corinthians, the apostle Paul expands this teaching with a memorable metaphor. That is the seed that is sown in the ground will be given its own appropriate shape and character when it springs to life, so the human body that is buried in the ground will be transformed at its rising again, having exchanged an earthly frame for a heavenly one. The body buried in the ground is a thing subject to corruption, to indignity, and to infirmity. The new body which rises to live again is incorruptible in its glory and its power.

This is the difference between the natural body which we inhabit on earth and the spiritual body which will be ours after the resurrection. Frail, defective, decaying earthly bodies cannot be ours in the eternal kingdom. Paul's prose rises to a climax of rare visionary splendor when he describes how the trumpet shall sound, the dead shall be raised, and what was mortal and corruptible shall be transformed into what is immortal and incorruptible (1 Cor 15:50-54). Such will be the final triumph over death, the ultimate snapping of the grave's long-held grip on the human race.

The Doctrine of Purgatory

We cannot pretend that the apostle Paul answers every one of the questions we would like to ask him on this tremendous subject. We are inclined to say to ourselves, "This sounds very grand and welcome for believers, this picture of a time when the graves will yield up their dead, and bodies fit for eternal habitation will be distributed to the faithful for their entry into bliss. But we must remember that Paul was writing nearly two thousand years ago, and we are still waiting for the last trumpet to sound. What about all the people who have died during the last twenty centuries? And what about me if I die tomorrow? Do I sleep away the years, centuries perhaps, until the time of Christ's Second Coming?"

Now here we have to admit that at this point the present book cannot continue to be written as though mainstream Christianity had one clearly agreed upon answer to our question. We have reached an area of speculation where even deeply committed Christians may find themselves in disagreement. What is the character of the intermediate state between a Christian's death tomorrow and the day of the Last Judgment when Christ will pass sentence on the whole human race? After all, our Lord's story of Dives and Lazarus presented a picture of one man wafted to heaven and another condemned to hell immediately after death before there could be any question of the Second Coming and a final separation of the world's sheep from its goats. Moreover, Christ himself promised one of the thieves crucified at his side that they would meet immediately after death in Paradise.

Catholic theology therefore has distinguished between the general judgment marking the end of the world, and the particular judgment marking the end of each individual life. There is no clearly defined account of what the particular judgment will be like, to match the Pauline pictures of the general judgment on the Last Day.

Nevertheless, Catholic teaching clearly envisions that the departed soul will be enabled after death to see itself as it is in the eyes of God. Saintly souls will then be admitted forthwith into the heavenly kingdom. Irretrievably lost souls will be straightaway condemned to hell. And sinners who are not irretrievably lost but who need to be cleansed before they are fit to enter into blessedness will go to purgatory. There they will be sanctified by purifying fire. That, at least, is the Catholic position.

St. Thomas Aquinas likens the experience of particular judgment after death to that of the hour of truth in which a person faces the supreme test of his courage at a time of desperate danger. There is such a moment for every man after death. He will be judged worthy of heaven and be admitted to glory. Or he will be judged unworthy and condemned to hell. Or he will be judged worthy of heaven but not yet fully prepared. If he is in the third category, he will be sent to purgatory to be purified and made fit for heaven.

Traditional Catholic teaching therefore does not provide a *real* third option. There remain only the two alternative destinations, heaven and hell. The third possibility is a delayed entry into heaven after due preparation.

Thus it is to purgatory that Catholic theology consigns the multitude of Christians who have lived in the fellowship of the church and benefited from sanctifying grace, but who go to their deaths encumbered with certain sins. In purgatory they will suffer as their sins are purged away. Catholic theologians have spoken of the great diversity of purgatorial suffering in both its intensity and its duration. But the Catholic church has accepted that prayers and masses offered on earth on behalf of departed souls can help to alleviate or abbreviate the sufferings of those souls in purgatory.

Purgatory therefore does not in the Catholic view offer a further chance after death for turning to God and gaining salvation. Only those who have already chosen God will have the purgational experience after death. Purgatory certainly provides the opportunity for the living to aid the dead, not in the sense of affecting their eternal destination, but in the sense of easing their way towards it.

It is perhaps better to call purgatory an interim state rather than an intermediate state since it is not a state between heaven and hell but a stage on the road to heaven.

Wide acceptance of belief in purgatory is of course a part of history. It is not surprising. We all accept that only the perfectly pure in heart can obtain the beatific vision. Reason encourages us to point to a fit immediate future after death for Christians we have known who have been faithful in many ways yet have carried their faults with them to the grave. We trust in God's mercy. Yet we cannot but feel that some process of purification will be necessary before they can expect to enter heaven. Indeed, knowing them as we do, we are sure that they themselves would want to undergo some costly process of purification.

Yet New Testament passages on the interim state seem to most Protestants naturally to imply that God's sanctifying purification is completed at the moment of death, so that when the body is left behind sinfulness is left behind, too. From this standpoint strong arguments can be brought against the whole concept of purgatory. In the first place, it can be said to understate the all-salvaging effect of Christ's redemptive act. Christ's saving work was finished on Calvary. The gift he offers us through his redeeming blood is a full and perfect forgiveness, a death to the old Adam, a new life in Christ. Insofar as we have responded in faith and love, we have entered upon resurrection life here and now. Final acceptance or rejection of Christ with the eternal consequence of either is precisely what human life on earth is all about.

In the second place, the doctrine of purgatory seems to lay an emphasis on the level of the individual's spiritual achievement which smacks of worldly ethicism to some Protestants. It seems to shift the balance of emphasis from faith to works. If we are saved by faith alone, taking a course in a posthumous penitentiary or even a reformatory school looks like an unnecessary supplement to what was achieved by Christ on Calvary. Indeed, Protestant theologians have argued that the doctrine of purgatory is founded on the barest of biblical texts. And it seems to conflict with the emphatic scriptural doctrine of salvation by faith alone. Christ's sacrifice frees us from sin. It is dangerous to encourage the illusion that men and women get some kind of progress report on earthly life which can be touched up after death.

And, in the third place, we cannot posit a postponement of entry into heaven without encouraging the notion of a second chance to get right with God. Such are the dangers which Protestants detect in the doctrine of purgatory.

Speculations about the interim or intermediate state have been argued about over the centuries. There are Christians who hold that between death and the Second Coming of Christ all souls are in a dreamless sleep. Knowing nothing of the passage of time and having no possibility of changing morally, they await simultaneous re-awakening at the judgment. There are those who believe in an intermediate state in which the unbelieving dead who have never rejected the gospel have the way opened to repentance and spiritual life. And there have been non-Catholic theologians who, far from rejecting the whole notion of purgatory, have believed in an intermediate state in which there will be a genuine second chance to respond savingly to God's saving action. But none of these ideas can claim clear Scriptural support.

Argument has often revolved around our Lord's words: "But whosoever speaketh against the Holy Ghost, it shall not be forgiven him, neither in this world, neither in the world to come" (Mt 12:32). They have been used by some to suggest that these are two opportunities to gain forgiveness; in this life, and after death. St. Augustine himself used the quotation as evidence that some of the dead will qualify *after* punishment to escape everlasting fire. In short, some will be pardoned in this world; and others, after punishment, will be pardoned in the next. It is important to recognize the *distinction* between delaying pardon so that it will not take effect until after purgation and giving human beings a second chance after death to make up for their failure to seek pardon on earth.

Disagreement on the subject of a possible intermediate or interim state is no doubt fueled by failure to shake off temporal habits of thinking when turning our minds to the afterlife. The very word interim has a time-bound connotation. In *The New Schaff-Herzog Encyclopedia of Religious Knowledge* (Editor S.M. Jackson, Grand Rapids, Michigan: Baker Book House, 1950), there is an article on purgatory by C.A. Beckwith which concludes:

> The difficulty that the detention of those who enter purgatory just previous to the final judgment is too short for purification is met by the suggestion that pure spirits are not under ordinary conditions of time, and that all things are present together in the eternity of God!

Just as it is illogical to talk of everlasting torment in times of ceaseless duration in a realm where notions of duration cease to be applicable, in the same way it is perhaps misleading to ask what happens *in the time* between death and the final judgment if we are dealing with a region outside time. Similarly, though we may picture a state of purgatory in which souls progress through a process of penance and purification, we must remind ourselves that in imposing temporal dimensions on that picture, we are taking imaginative liberties that are in some respects inadequate to what we are trying to portray. Can we really talk of personal development for the soul in purgatory with a definite beginning, middle, and end to the purification process?

Biblical teaching is about how to live in this world. The consequences of living well or badly in this world are presented only in generalizations and imagery. Indeed, sometimes a veil is drawn over the consequences. Our Lord tells the brief parable of the rich fool whose lands are so productive that he builds ever bigger granaries to hold ever bigger harvests until the time when he can say to himself, "Now I have all that I need for many years of comfortable life, eating, drinking, and making merry." The conclusion of the parable is a summary end to the man's life: "But God said unto him, Thou fool, this night thy soul shall be required of thee: then whose shall those things be, which thou hast provided?" (Lk 12:20).

Our Lord's only comment is, "So is he that layeth up treasure for himself, and is not rich toward God" (Lk 12:21). There is no direct mention of eternal punishment. It may be inferred that the rich fool gets what he deserves for being selfishly covetous and failing to acquire the spiritual wealth which God looks for in a man. That was the case with Dives. But Christ's emphasis here is on the sheer stupidity and shortsightedness of piling up treasure on earth.

Indeed, the parable sounds again the note heard in Christ's forecast of the Second Coming. Be on your guard. Be watchful. Take into your reckoning the fact that the end may come at any time. The unexpectedness of the individual's death is but a miniature of the unexpectedness of the Last Day.

It is reasonable for the Christian to assume that what God wants us to understand clearly will be clearly explained to us. That we are meant to shudder at the thought of hell is evident from the imagery of tormenting fire, of weeping and wailing and gnashing of teeth. That is how the prospect of hell is presented to us. That our hearts are meant to be lifted with delight and joy at the thought of heaven is equally clear from the imagery in which the prospect of heaven is presented to us. We will explore this imagery further in a later chapter. But we must remember that these sketchy accounts of the great alternatives are intended to touch the heart and rouse the will rather than to satisfy intellectual curiosity about what life beyond time will be like in concrete detail.

The Judgment to Come

What emerges most forcibly of all from Christ's teaching about the future is that judgment will come and that men and women need to be prepared for it. The theme is touched upon so many times and with such a variety of imagery that its centrality to our Lord's thinking cannot be doubted. And, in all cases, Christ represents himself as the one to pass ultimate authoritative judgment on the world.

He seems to be especially concerned to focus on this topic a richness of imagery which will impress by its vividness and touch the heart by its homeliness and familiarity. He compares himself to a thief breaking into a house at night (Mt 24:43) in order to stress the need for constant vigilance. He reminds his followers that the Second Coming will be like the downpour that flooded the world in the days of Noah in order to stress the need for constant preparedness (Mt 24:37-39).

In the extended parable of the talents, Christ compares himself to a wealthy nobleman who has to leave his estate for a time to visit a distant property. He delegates responsibility during his absence to ten servants, giving them ten pounds each as capital for trading. On his return the servant who has used the money and the time profitably is congratulated and promoted, while the servant who has hoarded what he was given and done nothing at all with it is punished.

The apostle Matthew's version of the story amplifies the commendation of the industrious servant with phrases that smack more of entry into heaven than of promotion to the board of directors: "Well done, thou good and faithful servant: ... enter thou into the joy of thy lord" (Mt 25:21). Similarly, the servant who has squandered his opportunities to invest is condemned in terms unmistakably awesome. "And cast ye the unprofitable servant into outer darkness: there shall be weeping and gnashing of teeth" (Mt 25:30). The lesson here is once more a solemn warning against misuse of the time before the Lord's return and a grave reminder of the terrible price to be paid for defaulting.

It is noticeable that in all these instances, as in the prophecy about the sheep and the goats and as in the story of Dives and Lazarus, it is not sins of commission *but* sins of omission that are under fire. The householder who fails to install burglar alarms and the revellers who fail to build boats against the flood are scarcely represented as villains. Even the unprofitable servant cannot, it appears, be charged either with embezzlement or with falsifying the estate's accounts. Yet their common inertia costs them dearly. The parable of the ten virgins also conveys a warning against unpreparedness, and in this case Christ presents himself as a bridegroom.

But there is one case where the theme of preparedness seems to be absent, and that is where Christ compares himself to a householder who sows good seed in his field. "But while men slept, his enemy came and sowed tares among the wheat, and went his way" (Mt 13:25). When wheat and tares grow up together and the householder's servants express their bewilderment, there is no question of a rebuke. The householder does not blame the men for having slept in their beds at night instead of organizing a rotation of night watchmen. He recognizes the hand of the enemy and declares that wheat and tares shall flourish undisturbed together until the harvest.

Then the reapers can garner the wheat into the barn, while the tares are bound in bundles and burnt (Mt 13:30). Christ's word-by-word elucidation of this parable leaves no room for doubt. The householder is the Son of man. The field is the world. The enemy who sows the tares is the devil. And the harvesting is the Last Judgment which will occur when the Son returns in glory with his angels. Those who commit iniquity the angels "shall cast into a furnace of fire," while the righteous shall "shine forth as the sun in the kingdom of their Father" (Mt 13:42-43).

What is especially heartwarming about this parable is that it seems designed precisely to comfort. Christ's followers are told not to worry about the fact that they live side by side with men and women corrupted by the devil yet seemingly flourishing in God's sun and rain as healthily as themselves. The day of reckoning will come and the policy of non-discrimination will be dropped. It will then be eternal sunshine for the righteous and the furnaces of hell for the wicked.

In view of the prominence of Christ's prophecies of the

Second Coming and the judgment it is not surprising that the theme of coming judgment is an essential element in the teaching of the Apostles. Nor is it surprising that many in the early church expected the Second Coming to occur in their own lifetimes. The apostle Paul, preaching at Athens, calls on all men to repent because God "hath appointed a day, in the which he will judge the world in righteousness by that man whom he hath ordained" (Acts 17:31).

And when the Roman governor Felix gives Paul, a captive in chains, the opportunity to explain his faith in Christ, what makes him tremble in his sandals is Paul's reasoning "of righteousness, temperance, and judgment to come" (Acts 24:25).

While the theme of coming judgment is constant in Paul's epistles, scholars have detected a change of emphasis from Paul's early assumption that our Lord will return in the not-too-distant future to a seemingly long-term concern with the building up of the church. The celebrated advice about marrying or not marrying given in 1 Corinthians (7:26-31) is delivered on the assumption that "the time is short" (v. 29) and that "the fashion of this world passeth away" (v. 31). No doubt this anticipation of a quick denouement of the world drama was a powerful incentive to urgent and rapid evangelization. Yet by the time John's Gospel was written the emphasis was more on the coming of the Holy Spirit than on the Second Coming of Christ.

"For the Father judgeth no man, but hath committed all judgment unto the Son," our Lord declares. He adds later that the Father has given him "authority to execute judgment also, because he is the Son of man" (Jn 5:22, 27). It is highly appropriate that the Son who has had personal experience of human life from the inside should be given the authority to pass judgment on humanity. But what is said in the apostle John's account between these two verses deserves to be pondered.

The Father has handed on to the Son the role of judge so that "all men should honor the Son, even as they honor the Father. He that honoreth not the Son honoreth not the Father which hath sent him" (Jn 5:23). In other words, it is by their response and attitude to the Son that men will be judged. On this basis, they will be granted eternal life. Christ presses the point home: "Verily, verily, I say unto you, He that heareth my word, and believeth on him that sent me, hath everlasting life, and shall not come into condemnation; but is passed from death unto life" (Jn 5:24).

Our Lord himself by his presence among men and women is not only the criterion by which righteousness can be measured, he is also the touchstone by which godliness can be tested. Christ comes among us and by the way we respond to him we reveal our character. Contact with Christ is thus in itself an ongoing process of judgment. In our daily decisions we are directly or indirectly responding positively through Christ to God and thereby passing from death to life. Or we are ignoring and implicitly rejecting God in Christ. We are thereby automatically condemned.

This is a matter well worth dwelling upon. We have grown accustomed to the thought that the incarnation is not just a one-time event—the entry of God into human flesh in Christ in the first century—but also a continuing reality in the life of the church and its members in all ages. We have learned to recognize that between Christ's first coming in the stable at Bethlehem and his Second Coming at the close of time, he makes daily incursions into the lives of his people. We have encounters with him whenever we pray or meditate, whenever we receive grace for our journey in the Eucharist, whenever we listen to his Word preached from the pulpit. We encounter him whenever we catch a glimpse of one of those people in need that he himself mentioned—the sick who might be comforted, the poor who might be aided, the imprisoned who might be visited.

By the response we make on each of these occasions, we measure ourselves against the criterion of his loving mercy, we test ourselves against the touchstone of his holy obedience to the Father. In other words, we are continually facing judgment. Like the reality of God Incarnate which is daily renewed in the lives of the faithful, the coming divine judgment is daily anticipated in the lives of all men and women.

If it is true that for practical purposes we are daily under judgment, daily equipping ourselves for heaven or for hell, then something else would seem to follow logically from this. It is quite simply that if we are men and women of any spiritual sensitivity then we are daily getting an anticipatory taste of heaven or hell.

If this is the case, it would be wrong to view Christ's final judgment of us as a cataclysmic event puncturing the tenor of humanity's story like a sudden thunderclap and cutting across the grain of our growth and development. Rather Christ's final judgment of us will represent the culminating stage of a long sequence of daily choices made over a lifetime. Some of the choices—perhaps the most influential ones—will have been choices made at moments of crisis after tense inner conflict. Others will have flowed from these key choices by repetitive habit established for good or ill.

It is appropriate to think of the Last Judgment as a great turning of tables in the sense that the rich in the things of this world and the Lazaruses of this world are in for quite a shock when they discover that their roles have been reversed. The road of thoughtlessly indulged plenty and comfort has led to privation and torment, while the road of beggarly want and suffering has led to blessedness and peace. But it is not appropriate to talk of the Last Judgment as a great turning of tables in respect to the real inner lives of men and women.

Rather, the Last Judgment simply reveals to them what they have been after in their earthly lives, what they have made of themselves. Have they been choosing self and ignoring God? This fact is realized and made permanent in their being completely shut off from God in total, unrelieved involvement with an angry, unregenerate self. Did they at any point turn in a wholehearted way from the path of self-serving strategies to embrace Christ as their Lord and Savior, and live for God henceforth? Have they been, for all their moments of failure and weakness, for the most part steadily trying to serve God and love him? Very well. This underlying orientation of the will and the heart is fulfilled and made permanent in their entry into God's presence and the kingdom of the blessed.

Eternal life will be to that extent all of a piece with life in time. The freedom we have been given here below by God seems an awesome and onerous gift indeed when we reckon what its exercise can win for us, what its abuse can cost us. Seventy years of earthly life in time may seem a small and fleeting experience when measured against an eternity of bliss. But seventy years of earthly life in time assumes an immense weight of meaning when it is seen as the period during which an eternity of bliss may be won or lost.

Yet, in fact, neither the word winning nor the word losing is quite right. You run a race to win a silver cup. When you run too slowly you lose the cup. But the relationship between our earthly pilgrimage and the heaven or the hell that it brings us is not the relationship between a test in a certain form of activity and a reward in the form of some object or status. The relationship between our earthly pilgrimage and our eternal destiny is such that the eternal destiny will be a just and right fulfillment of that pilgrimage with all the marks of its good or ill intensified and made permanent.

Judgment Now

It may be that we Christians ought to become much more conscious of divine judgment already at work in our lives. The pulling back of the future upon the present does not after all require of us a great deal of mental effort. We are already aware of how time is transcended in the operation of God's works on earth. We do not hesitate to thrust the present back upon the past in dwelling on Christ's crucifixion. We do not imagine that we are any less the beneficiaries of his redemptive act than were his contemporaries. We sing hymns which make nonsense of time's tyranny in this respect. A well-known hymnist, Mrs. C.F. Alexander, wrote a moving hymn for Good Friday called: "Forgive them, O my Father." It contains the verse:

> It was my pride and hardness
> That hung him on the Tree;
> Those cruel nails, O Savior,
> Were driven in by me.

Every time we sing in hymns or speak in prayers of Christ's sacrifice lifting the burden of our sins, or of our sins having their part in the mass of human sinfulness that led to Christ's crucifixion—we cancel out all natural thinking in terms of time-bound cause and effect. We make ourselves partly responsible for events that happened two thousand years ago. We make the events of two thousand years ago directly relevant to millions of sins not then committed and to millions of sinners not then born.

The old seventeenth century Latin hymn translated as "My God, I love thee; not because / I hope for heaven thereby" contains the lines:

> Thou, O my Jesus, thou didst me
>   Upon the Cross embrace;
> For me didst bear the nails and spear,
>   And manifold disgrace.

> And griefs and torments numberless,
>   And sweat of agony;
> Yea, death itself—and all for me
>   Who was thine enemy.

We rightly thus think of what happened on Good Friday and Easter Day as something more than historical events of crucial importance for the rest of time. We see them as events transcending historical time. And thus we can justly picture ourselves held in Christ's embrace on the cross or justly number ourselves among the enemies who killed him. We helped to drive in the nails. Then we were embraced in forgiveness among those who knew not what they did.

This kind of supra-temporal thinking becomes natural to Christians. Since time is contained within eternity and history is held in the hands of God, we must expect that God's management of the world and his overt interventions in the human drama will shake men and women out of the straitjacket of limited time-bound thinking. Whenever we make a statement about God's nature we jump mentally out of our temporal skins. We say, "God is love" or "God is just." We are thereby expressing a view to which our sense of time is irrelevant. Suppose someone said to us "Do you also believe that God *was* just last century as well and *will be* just in the next century too?" We should be astonished that anyone should so misunderstand the eternal context of statements about God.

We cannot reflect on the doctrines of Christ's incarnation, the atonement, and the redemption without breaking free of the fetters of limitedly temporal thinking. Similarly we cannot reflect on the doctrine of creation without breaking free of those fetters. The doctrine of creation does not just tell us that in far-off prehistory God made the world and all that is in it. It isn't as though when the task was completed there was no more to be done and God could turn his attention elsewhere. We do not localize God's creativity in the dim and distant recesses of the past. We do not in our hymns just thank God for setting the life of the universe in motion. We thank him for everything that is *present* around us. In another of Mrs. C.F. Alexander's hymns, "All things bright and beautiful," we sing:

Each little flower that opens,
    Each little bird that sings,
He made their glowing colours,
    He made their tiny wings.

And we go on to thank him for every sunset and dawn, every winter and summer, and for "the rushes by the water / We gather every day." In short, we mentally pull forward God's creative action to cover everything that is around us today in God's good creation, millions of centuries after the forming of the universe.

If we focus thus upon God's creative acts and God's redemptive acts as ever-present in their effects, ever-relevant to our lives in time, why are we so reluctant to focus too upon our Lord's final coming in judgment as ever-relevant to our daily doings? In the hymn book in which I have just looked up Mrs. Alexander's hymns, the index puts the hymns in their appropriate groupings such as Christmas, Easter, The Holy Spirit, Harvest, and Saints' Days. Among over a hundred headings and sub-headings I could find no reference to judgment. Among the six hundred and thirty hymns three were listed under the category of the Second Coming.

Now it may not be fair to rush too quickly to the conclusion that there is a lack of balance here, for there are hymns which touch incidentally on judgment. When we sing "Come, ye thankful people, come" at harvest time, we quickly move in thought from the harvesting of earthly crops to our Lord's final harvesting of human souls:

> For we know that thou wilt come,
> And wilt take thy people home;
> From thy field wilt purge away
> All that doth offend, that day;
> And thine angels charge at last
> In the fire the tares to cast,
> But the fruitful ears to store
> In thy garner evermore.

But mentally we locate this climactic separation of the righteous from the wicked at a comfortably distant date. We are less likely to bring back to our consciousness of the present the awesome facts of God's judgment than we are to pull forward upon our consciousness of the present the delightful truth of God's creation and the comforting knowledge of Christ's redemption of his people.

From the eternity in which God dwells, he has put the pressure of his finger upon the course of temporal history in various degrees of clarity. Were the print of his hands not recognized by mankind there would be no Christian religion. That means that for us there would be nothing but a sequence of days and years beginning—if we are lucky—in animal vitality and ending in decay and death. All that gives meaning to our earthly vocation derives from beyond time. God has actual and spoken, visited and redeemed his people. So doing, he has stamped a pattern of meaning upon the otherwise purposeless flux of physical growth and decay which would constitute human life.

That pattern of meaning transfigures temporal things in the light of the eternal. At the center of this long story of divine nourishment of the creatures he has made lies the supreme entry of the Creator into his creation. God made his divine entry into history in the incarnate life of Christ and the redemptive act of self-sacrifice on the cross. At the ultimate moment of self-offering our Lord declared, "It is finished." The divine task was completed. But human history was by no means finished. And however many centuries human history lasts, they cannot but focus the lives and destinies of ever more and more people on that crucial event.

Ancient and modern poets have defined Christ's cross as the *axletree* on which the world of human history revolves. It is an apt image for conveying the crucial centrality of Christ's redemptive act in the whole human drama. The image encourages our minds to escape from that picture of human history in a straight-line sequence which is so limiting to our thinking. We do not move forward like railroad cars on a steel track, forever leaving stations, signal boxes, and telephone poles behind, never to be re-experienced for a moment in our journey through time. Human history may flow like a river, but what gives shape to human lives is what is both within history and beyond it, within time and outside it, like Christ's death and rising.

In our baptism and in whatever life of Christian commitment we achieve, the stamp of those events is imprinted on our personalities as it was imprinted on the personalities of the apostles Peter and Paul. Faithful Christians carry about with them the marks of Christ's incarnate life and the redemption he won for them. Jesus Christ was alive in the days of Herod and Pilate. He is alive now and forevermore. We are told that insofar as we live fruitfully we live in him.

Although chronological time is transcended in all our relationships with Christ, nevertheless history flows by on its irreversible course, and this is the dimension in which our animal lives are wholly contained. As intelligent bipeds we were born and we shall die. Time is not a human invention. It is God's invention. He holds history in his grasp, all times are in his hands, and the breath of the eternal Spirit blows through our beings if we let it. Nevertheless the human drama had a beginning and it will have an end. And this is the precise reason why we cannot afford to neglect thinking about the Last Day. Indeed, reflection on the Second Coming and the Last Day is an important safeguard against having our thinking about creation subtly secularized. For the converse of the creation of the universe is the winding-down of the universe. The divine hand that set the human drama in motion will ring down the curtain on it in the end.

Forget or discount the Second Coming and the judgment, and the doctrine of divine creation loses its tremendous force and significance. Being hazy and weak on the doctrine of the Second Coming and the coming judgment will make us hazy and weak on the doctrine of creation. For it is the end of a scheme, that is its purpose and conclusion, which gives meaning to its beginning. Without emphasis on the ultimate end of man, his beginning loses its momentousness. If the ultimate purpose of creation is not present to the mind, then creation becomes a beginning in the sense that one day you start shaving, instead of a beginning in the sense that one day you start to build a house.

Some evolutionists tell us that the universe has developed by chance. Christians say that God created it. So far as the here-and-now is concerned, does it matter which? Only insofar as God created it *with a purpose*; which means, only insofar as the God who created it intends one day to bring it to an end. Indeed, unless we remain firmly aware of the end of the world (the *end* in both senses, purpose and conclusion), our thinking about creation is likely to be subtly secularized. I'm secular nation in any sphere of thought overlooks and dispenses with ultimate purpose.

There is more than one way of reflecting on the judgment. I recall several years ago receiving typically generous American hospitality from a couple who were certainly born-again Christians, though I did not inquire what their denomination was. They were showing me the beauty of the Massachusetts coastline when my host at the steering wheel suddenly turned to me and asked "Do you often think about the Second Coming?"

"Frankly, no," I said. Then naturally I asked, "Do you?"

"Oh yes," he said, "a lot. I'm always picturing it." And he went on to speak eloquently about how he relished the prospect of himself and his wife, his children and his grandchildren, all being swept into the company of the elect to dwell in light and glory, while the poor sinners and unbelievers scurried off in search of shelter from the wrath to come.

I was taken aback. I did not know whether to be envious of his confidence or critical of his complacency. We have already seen that in Christ's actual prophecy of the Second Coming there is a great deal that does not encourage you to rub your hands in jolly anticipation. The consolatory prospect of the Son of man coming in the clouds with great glory is preceded by frightening prophecies of false Christs in plenty, wars and natural disasters, persecution, strife, and treachery within families, and desolation and affliction of all kinds.

On the other hand as the judgment complements the creation, so the second Advent complements the first Advent. The coming of Christ ought not to be dreaded by any Christian. The God who came in the first place as the babe of Bethlehem is not going to come to the human race he so honored and loved as an ogre of vengeance. Let me quote one of the sermons which the distinguished English theologian Austin Farrer collected in his book, *The Crown of the Year* (London, England: Dacre Press, A & C Black Ltd., 1952) He provides a one-paragraph sermon for every Sunday in the church's year. This is the one for the Second Sunday in Advent when the gospel for the day was the apostle Luke's account of the Second Coming (Lk 21:25-33):

Advent brings Christmas, judgment runs out into mercy. For the God who saves us and the God who judges us is one God. We are not, even, condemned by his severity and redeemed by his compassion; what judges us is what redeems us, the love of God. What is it that will break our hearts on judgment day? Is it not the vision, suddenly unrolled, of how he has loved the friends we have neglected, of how he has loved us, and we have not loved him in return; how, when we came before his altar, he gave us himself, and we gave him half-penitences, or resolutions too weak to commit our wills? But while love thus judges us by being what it is, the same love redeems us by effecting what it does. Love shares flesh and blood with us in this present world, that the eyes which look us through at last may find in us a better substance than our vanity.

When Austin Farrer writes "while love thus judges us by being what it is," he is saying, rather more neatly and concisely, what I said a few pages back when I wrote: "Our Lord himself, in his presence among men and women, is not only the criterion by which righteousness can be measured, he is also the touchstone by which godliness can be tested." In pulling together Christ's coming at Bethlehem, his coming in the Eucharist, and his final coming, Dr. Farrer implies that his love is always present with us in judgment as well as in redemption. Farrer's final image is an impressive one—the idea that the sacramental body and blood are the only really solid nourishment we get on earth, in that they build us up with real inner substance which will prevent us from being empty to the eyes of the divine Judge.

Time and Eternity

At several points in this book so far, it has been necessary to remind the reader that to consider things eternal from a standpoint within time is to attempt something that human minds are not fully equipped for. We find it almost impossible to escape from thinking in terms of time. There is no harm in that, for that is how God made us. But Christian theology, by virtue of its subject matter, requires us to make some effort to escape this limitation.

There is no sun and moon in heaven and none in hell either. The concepts of eternal day and eternal night preclude all earthly notions of temporal movement and change. The apostle Paul's insistence that our resurrection bodies will be immortal and incorruptible has far-reaching implications. It is difficult for us to conceive of existence in bodies which do not age. Our whole outlook on life is shot through with notions of growth and change.

The baby becomes a child. The child becomes a young man or woman. The young man or woman becomes middle-aged. Then the middle-aged become old. Moreover, our short lifespan is locked into a system of sequence and cycle which characterizes the earth we live in. The old die and are buried in the ground. From the same ground grows the grain which feeds the next generation. From the same ground grows the grass which feeds the cows which provide the milk which nourishes the baby and the infant. The seed is buried in the ground, and grain springs up for harvest. The ram's seed is buried in the ewe in winter, and lambs are born in spring. The man's seed is planted in the woman, and a baby is born three quarters of a year later.

The total system of cycles of growth and decay, birth and breeding and death, belong strictly to our life in time. So deeply does it permeate our thinking that we find it virtually impossible to think of timeless existence. When we try to picture an afterlife, we inevitably insinuate notions of growth and development according to earthly standards which fall short of the mark.

What is there is help us to conceive of the difference between a time-locked sphere and a timeless one? We can perhaps begin to imagine what temporal existence looks like from an eternal standpoint by recalling our experience of reading books or seeing plays and films. We read a historical novel about men and women caught up in their twenties and thirties in World War I. Life stories pass before our eyes. Late nineteenth century childhoods and school days, early twentieth century exploits in young manhood and young womanhood, perhaps railway journeys across Europe or voyages in liners across the Atlantic. Then we watch the young men called up for military service in a totally different sphere of activity. There are accounts of trench life, bombardments, battles, and deaths. We share emotionally the hopes and dreams, disappointments and agonies of men and women over the whole pattern of their days. Yet the total sequence is compressed into only a few hours of reading. And not only do decades of human experience pass through our minds in a few hours, but we are detached from the temporal sequence and impose on the picture of a man dying in battle the picture of a schoolboy who once played cowboys and Indians in the school playground.

This may aid us in trying to imagine what life on earth looks like in God's eyes. There is no doubt that we exercise our imagination in very complex ways when we experience books or plays or films. Perhaps we go to the theater to see Shakespeare's *Julius Caesar*. We are transported back to the first century B.C. to watch events leading up to the assassination of Caesar and the dire consequences for the assassins.

So here we are sitting in our theater in the 1980s, watching a re-enactment of events in February and March 44 B.C. when the conspirators Cassius and Brutus plotted and accomplished the assassination of Rome's greatest general in his hour of triumph. But from time to time we catch a phrase or a reference which reminds us that the man who wrote the play did so in the sixteenth century during the reign of Queen Elizabeth I. Thus, we impose on the picture we receive of life in Rome in the first century B.C. notions of life in Elizabethan London in the sixteenth century A.D.

Perhaps, after all, it is not beyond our powers to conceive of a standpoint in eternity from which history can be seen to unfold before the eyes. Even the future of a kind passes before our eyes when we read science fiction about what is to come. And when we read George Orwell's *1984* today, we go through the complicated mental process of reminding ourselves that events represent a forecast of a future projected some thirty years before it came to pass. Yet that same future is now our past!

Christians have to learn not to allow their thinking to be time-ridden. We do not lack aids to assist us in shaking off the fetters of time's dominion. I dream one night of life in my family as it was twenty years ago. There is my son behaving with perfect naturalness and there is my wife behaving with perfect naturalness. It is only when I wake up and recall the dream that I realize what nonsense it was in temporal terms.

At the time when we lived in the house in question, my son was ten years old and his wife—who joined us in the dream there—never saw the place and was unknown to us while we lived there. Moreover, now that I look back analytically on the dream I realize that my son was managing to be at one and the same time a boy of ten and a young man of thirty. He was a boy coming home from school and a family man with a wife and a daughter. The appearance of my father among the shifting sequences was even more absurd, for he died before this son was even born and before ever we lived in the city where the dream was set.

The blending of past and present in dreams is not unusual. That is the dreamworld, we say, meaning that it is an unreal and fanciful projection by the mind. So it seems to hindsight, but the interesting thing about the blending or merging of different periods of life is that the merger is totally convincing within the context of the dream itself. I do not suggest that this merging of widely separated years of our life in dreams is some kind of escape to a more real world than the living one. But it gives us an experience which is immensely helpful when we try to rid ourselves of slavery to time in thinking about what is eternal.

There remain mental obstacles in the way of straight thinking about eternity. They impede us when we face what are two of the most difficult questions of all about the afterlife, namely: "How could God allow anyone to be tormented unendingly?" and "What happens to the individual between the day of death and the resurrection of the body on the Last Day?" Neither of them is a straight question because to talk of being tormented unendingly and to talk of a period of the afterlife between death and the Last Day is to introduce into our thinking about eternity, notions of duration which can be applicable only within the finite world of time.

FIVE

Heaven and Earth

What is Heaven Like?

Suppose you have a position in some enterprise in which perhaps score or hundreds of others are involved. Suppose, say, you belong to the chorus of a major opera company. You are asked to speak or to write about your experiences. You have a fund of anecdotes. You can talk at length about the difficulties of launching yourself on a musical career, the tests you passed to get into a music college, the tests you underwent to get into the opera company, the difficulties you had in keeping your place.

Your whole story is colored by accounts of the companions who failed to get into the music college, or into the opera company, or who failed to keep their places there. So-and-so's voice did not develop as it was expected to do. So-and-so's sight-reading proved to be not nearly good enough. So-and-so's magnificent voice could not be exploited because he could never be relied upon to sing in tune. Or perhaps your recollections turn to the difficulties in backstage conditions. They were never properly remodelled when the company expanded. Now they have deteriorated. Dry-rot has invaded a row of dressing rooms, and some prima donnas have thrown tantrums about it, demanding greater luxury under threat of walking out.

Anecdotes are legion concerning singers, orchestral players, managers, costumiers, scenery designers, producers, box-office staff, lighting technicians, front-office personnel, and all the rest. Your reminiscences could fill a book or hold an

107

audience fascinated for hours. At the end a reader or a listener may complain, "You've entranced me. Some of your stories of people who never made it in the opera world or were sacked from it are the stuff of tragedy. Some of your tales of how this or that went wrong on stage or off stage are hilarious. But you have given us no account of a fully successful performance of *Aida* or *La Bohème* or *Carmen* or any other work. Surely that is what an opera company is all about."

It is indeed. And, talk as we may of hundreds of other matters, heaven is what Christianity is all about.

To begin with, heaven is where God dwells. "Our Father, who art in heaven," Christ taught us to pray. We are to recall where God is when we address him. It might have been otherwise, might it not? "When ye pray, say, Omnipotent God who art present everywhere, permeating all creation . . ." Yet it is a Father in heaven we are taught to pray to and a kingdom of heaven we are invited to enter.

Heaven is where God dwells and where dwell other beings, whether of human stock or not, who enjoy eternal bliss. The Lord's prayer wastes no words. It is concise and economical. But it contains a second clear reference to heaven. "Thy will be done, in earth as it is in heaven." Heaven is where everything is as it should be. It provides the criterion of all fitness and rightness. Heaven is where the drama of divine Creation begins and heaven is where it ends. Hell is defined by its total rejection of the heavenly. Earth is defined by its attempt to some extent, and by its failure for the most part, to be heavenly.

For the apostle Paul the whole creation is groaning and heaving like a woman in labor. It exists now in a state of joyful anticipation but of painful preparation. For real life begins for the sons of God only when creation and creature are delivered "from the bondage of corruption" (KJV), "from its bondage to decay" (RSV), into "the glorious liberty of the children of God" (Rom 8:21-22). On this view, what we know of life so far has been one long, uncomfortable preparation, one long experience of dragging around the burden of pregnancy, one long sequence of disaster-fraught rehearsals for a performance that has yet to be put on.

Concepts of achieving freedom from bondage to corruption and decay and of entering upon a state of glorious liberty shift the direction of our everyday thinking. Creatures of earth, we inevitably make earthly experience a measure of reality. We have no other option open to us. There are intellectual and spiritual equivalents of the physical law of gravity. Attention, desire, and aspiration focus naturally on the things of earth, homes to be built and dwelt in, clothes to be manufactured and worn, children to be born and reared.

Now it is true that all the effort and achievement involved in these activities may in the long run lead nowhere, in the sense that our universe is running down. But with our limited span of human perception, we cannot be much impressed by the fact that millions and millions of ages hence the universe may have burnt itself out. The scientific theory which foresees such a finality is after all a very abstract one. It can have little relevance to today's concrete concerns with bringing up the children, arranging the daily meals, and repairing the leaky roof.

A seventeenth century English poet, Henry Vaughan, once meditated on some verses in the First Epistle of John:

> For all that is in the world, the lust of the flesh, and the lust of the eyes, and the pride of life, is not of the Father, but is of the world. And the world passeth away, and the lust thereof: but he that doeth the will of God abideth forever. (1 Jn 2:16-17)

Vaughan then wrote a poem called "The World" in which he pictured lovers, statesmen, misers, and epicures whirled around in darkness, seemingly preferring the blackness of night to the true day:

> I saw Eternity the other night
> Like a great ring of pure and endless light.

Thus the poem begins, and it illustrates the difficulty of giving body and form, flesh and blood, to the contrast between the things of earthly life and the things of God's eternity. A ring of light such as Vaughan dreamed of may make a very fine spectacle indeed. But it would be fair for the secularly minded critic to point out that you cannot feed the next generation on rings of light, nor can you carry out Christ's injunction to aid the needy if rings of light are all you have to offer them.

I am trying to tackle a difficult question. It is accepted that we have to learn to set our hearts on things above rather than on things here about us on the earth. It is accepted that this earthly life is a transient experience which ends for all in physical death. It is accepted that the heaven where God dwells is eternal and that he has destined us to share it with him. All these clear truths of Christian teaching assert a primacy for the heavenly over the earthly which produces outbursts such as the apostle John's and Henry Vaughan's. In short, as we have said, heaven is what Christianity is all about. Yet, you will say, heaven is not what earthly life can ever be all about. For earthly life is about earning one's keep, finding somewhere to live, equipping children for the next school year, and paying the gas and electricity bills.

We must not imagine that giving heaven its due place in our thinking means dreaming of rings of light when we ought to be doing the dishes. When our Lord turned his attention to the kingdom of heaven in his teaching, he did not speak of rings of light. We have his authority for picturing heaven in terms of earthly human activities—such as a wedding feast. Does this mean that no dividing line can be drawn between activities proper to earth and activities proper to heaven? Clearly there can be no sin in heaven and no ugliness, nothing that deceives and nothing that decays. And clearly there need be nothing in heaven to compensate for physical difficulties and defects which are aspects of earthly life.

We have biblical authority for picturing ourselves seated at a banquet in heaven; but presumably, wherever the banquet is held, there will be no need for central heating or air conditioning or roof repairs. All the paraphernalia of protection against rain and wind, snow and ice, will surely be unnecessary. Raincoats and umbrellas, gloves and winter boots are all of the earth.

But once you start to dispense with the paraphernalia of earth in picturing heaven, where do you stop? Clocks and watches would obviously be redundant. Vacuum cleaners and lawn mowers would obviously be unnecessary. Yet if that banquet is to be eaten decently, knives and forks and spoons must be available. Also, if the menu is to come up to heavenly standards, there must surely be pots and pans and mixers somewhere in the background.

The truth is that we shall get ourselves into a nonsensical tangle if we carry all earth's imagery with us into our attempt to picture heaven. Likewise, we shall end up with a featureless Nirvana if we try to scrap all earth's imagery before picturing heaven. Moreover, we shall lose ourselves in absurdities if we try to distinguish between equipment appropriate for heaven and equipment totally inappropriate. Traditionally, voices and harps have been imaged to supply music in heaven, not juke boxes or electric guitars. The blest have been pictured in white robes, not in T-shirts or jeans. To some extent this is due to the fact that the great painters of the Renaissance portrayed heaven in an idiom of idealized contemporaneity, and the influence of their work lingers with us.

We have to try to clear our minds on the two questions: In what respect does heavenly life contrast with earthly life? In what respect does heavenly life resemble earthly life? The contrasting aspects are obvious. The apostle Paul put his finger on some of them. The earthly is subject to corruption and decay. Insofar as it has life, it grows, blooms, withers, and dies. Human, animal, and vegetable life share the same fate. "The flower that blooms today / Tomorrow dies." From the time of the psalmist onwards, poets have lamented the transience of earthly joy, earthly beauty, earthly life itself. By contrast heaven is the place of what is perfect, flawless, and incorruptible. Nothing there can fade or die. It lasts eternally. The contrast is between what is sure, reliable, and unchanging, and what is mutable, untrustworthy, and fleeting.

But it has to be noticed that some of the insecure, unreliable, fading, and shifting aspects of earthly experience have a positive as well as a negative element. You would not complain because an attack of influenza is a short-lived experience. You would not complain because a stomachache is here today and gone tomorrow.

I once heard a woman reflecting on her past experience of grave mental illness of an acutely depressing kind. "There was one thing about it which prevented it from being totally intolerable," she said. "However black the despair, there was knowledge in the back of the mind that it would terminate and I would recover." There is a real sense in which earthly experience shelters us from unbearable agony. The suddenly bereaved widower or widow says to himself or herself, "Life is empty. It will never be the same again. But there will at least be in time a degree of recovery from this present sense of total misery and desperation."

It is the good things of life whose passing we lament. "Fair daffodils, we weep to see / You haste away so soon," wrote the poet Robert Herrick. Indeed, the poets of all ages lament the way youth decays into age, beauty fades, and love dies. It is the things which to our minds make earth like heaven whose passing away we deeply regret. John Keats, a poet much obsessed by the transience of youth and beauty and love—no doubt the more acutely so because of his own consumptive condition—lamented that a note of melancholy impinges on all human experiences of beauty, joy, and delight, because we know that these experiences cannot last.

The notion that earthly joy can never be wholly unalloyed because there is always consciousness of its fleetingness at the back of the mind is perhaps the product of a peculiarly pagan outlook. For the Christian, surely the joys tasted and lost here below are to be fully recovered and renewed in heaven.

For what can heavenly joy involve if not the recovery, intensification, and immortalization of all that is good and beautiful in earthly life? Of course, it will involve much more than that too, much that is outside the scope of earthly understanding and indeed beyond the reach of earthly aspiration. But insofar as we have been given senses and brains to experience what is good here below, we have surely been granted the opportunity for foretastes of heaven. After all, we are told that God made man in his own image. We are not specifically told that God made the earth in heaven's image. But logically the latter follows from the former. As men and women, we cannot think of human life, of human experience, except in an appropriate environment.

Our eyesight would be useless or non-existent if there were nothing to look at—no shapes, colors, lights, and shades. Our hearing would be inert or non-existent if there were nothing to listen to—no human voices, no songbirds, no music, no sound of moving wind or water. Our sense of smell would be non-existent if there were no perfume from flowers, savory odors from cooking food, or fragrance from the fresh air.

Now it is pointless to speculate what God himself has in place of eyes and ears, nose and teeth. In the same way it is idle to speculate on what the heavenly equivalent would be of surveying the countryside from a mountaintop or enjoying a plate of pork chops. The apostle Paul has told us that we are to be raised in new bodies as appropriate to the realm of the incorruptible as our present bodies are appropriate to the realm of the corruptible.

Nevertheless the interaction of the human being and his environment is of the essence of his humanity. If this is so and man is made in God's image, it would seem to follow that there is at least some faint reflection in our earthly environment of what, for want of a better term, we must call God's heavenly environment. In short, theologians and poets have not been exercising their imaginations improperly when they have pictured our earthly environment as imaging the heavenly one. The apostle John gave us the lead in this respect when he pictured the glorious new Jerusalem come down from heaven in the Book of Revelation.

In Milton's *Paradise Lost* the archangel Raphael visits Adam and Eve in the Garden of Eden. He warns Adam of the need for obedience. In his innocence, Adam is bewildered by the warning. It is surely impossible to conceive of disobedience to a God who has given Eve and Adam everything that could be desired. Raphael replies that God wants a voluntary, not an automatic response from his creatures. The angels in heaven themselves enjoy their happiness on the basis of willing, not compulsory, obedience. "Freely we serve / Because we freely love," Raphael tells the father of our race (PL, 5:538).

To emphasize the point, Raphael concedes that some angels have already experimented with disobedience and have been cast down from heaven to hell as a consequence. The mention of the fall of the angels arouses Adam's curiosity. He wants to know all about it. The archangel agrees to tell him. But first he must warn of the difficulty of relating to the human under-standing the "invisible exploits / Of warring Spirits." I shall have to use earthly analogies, Raphael says, and then adds this significant afterthought:

> Though what if Earth
> Be but a shadow of Heaven, and things therein
> Each to other like, more than on earth is thought?
> (PL 5:574)

In other words, suppose the earth is the reflection of heaven. Suppose things on earth resemble things in heaven more closely than earthly beings imagine.

Escape from Time

We have seen how poets in all ages have lamented the transience of the good things in earthly life—beauty fading, the rose withering, youth decaying into age. These are of course essentially the effects of time. But the promise of the gospel is of everlasting life. It would seem to follow that a key difference between earthly life and heavenly life is the escape from the dimension of time. As soon as we try to imagine the good things of life made permanent and unfading, we find our minds stretched beyond their capacities.

To begin with, so many of the pleasures of life depend upon movement in time. The summer holiday is enjoyed because it gives us a total change from our routine daily activities through most of the year. But we should find it boring if it went on for a lifetime. There is pleasure at the end of the holiday in returning to the work we so gladly put down when our vacation began. To rest and sleep when we are tired is no less desirable than to wake and stir into action when we have been refreshed by sleep. Quite apart from the absurdity of trying to imagine ourselves permanently eating our favorite ice cream or permanently staring at the sunset over the Grand Canyon, even the more sophisticated and intellectualized delights such as gazing at beautiful pictures or reading great literature or listening to musical masterpieces make their impact upon us by being intermittent experiences. They are enjoyed for an hour or two and then are gone.

But clearly it would be illogical to imagine life out of time as rendering this or that particular pleasure permanent. There would be no opportunity to relish quietness and peace if you were seated at an everlasting symphony concert. Although you might be permanently eating your favorite ice cream at the same time as your favorite Mahler symphony meandered on unceasingly, there would surely be delights impossible to combine with an eternal orchestral performance.

If one of the great joys of earthly life lies in the variety of delights we are offered, then variety cannot be excluded from what is to be enjoyed in heaven. So if we do not yearn to escape from an existence in which this pleasure terminates as that pleasure begins, in which holidays and symphonies have ends as well as beginnings, what are the limitations of life in time which we long to cast aside?

Surely the limitation of life in time which we long most

earnestly and sincerely to escape from is the experience of loss. There is no sense of loss when the last chords of the symphony have been played, or we should not immediately begin to applaud the conductor. There is no sense of loss when the last moist sweetness of the ice cream we have consumed has slipped away from the tongue. We have listened to a moving musical performance. There is pleasure in its completeness. We have enjoyed the flavor of a favorite treat. There is satisfaction in what has been relished.

There would be a keen sense of loss only if it were known that one of these experiences could never be repeated. If deafness afflicted you and you had to say to yourself "No more music," or if you became diabetic and had to say to yourself "No more ice cream," then, indeed, there would be a real sense of loss. But of course the passage of time, even if it does not eventually produce deafness, desensitizes human responses in so many ways.

No one at the age of fifty can take the same rapturous delight in his thirtieth hearing of Beethoven's fifth symphony that he took in his first half-dozen hearings in his teens and early twenties. And the palate likewise gets desensitized. In our fifties, we can hurry past the candy shop which would have lured our eyes to its window in childhood.

There is a celebrated little poem, "Jenny Kissed Me," by Leigh Hunt. The poet expresses sudden joy in his advancing years because a young girl has jumped up from her seat on his entry into a room and kissed him spontaneously. "I may weary, I may be sad, I may be growing old," he says; but "Jenny kissed me":

Jenny kissed me when we met,
Jumping from the chair she sat in.
Time, you thief, who love to get
Sweets into your list, put that in.

Now the interesting thing here is the way the poet spontaneously addresses time as a thief who collects good things and then presumably makes off with them. It was not an original image. Something very much like it appears in Shakespeare's play *Troilus and Cressida:*

> Time hath, my lord, a wallet at his back
> Wherein he puts alms for oblivion.

Time is here a travelling beggar with a great bag on his back. Anything he gets his hands on is thrown into it to be forgotten forever.

If time did not take things away from us we should not lament being subject to time. But it bereaves us of loved ones, it takes away our youthful vitality and health, and leaves us with age's weariness and decrepitude. Little by little it impairs the finer reactions of the senses. And not always little by little. I have just read in the daily newspaper some paragraphs from a new book by a celebrated English novelist, Brigid Brophy, who has been stricken with multiple sclerosis in her mid-fifties. "It is an illness that inflicts awareness of loss," she writes. "I have in part died in advance of the total event." Yet she seems to recognize that the affliction merely exaggerates and intensifies a deprivation which time effects anyway, illness or no illness. "Yet the past is, except through memory and imagination, irrecoverable in any case, whether or not your legs are strong enough to sprint after it" (*The Times* (London), February 12, 1987).

The irrecoverability of the past, however, is surely one of those aspects of life in time from which life in eternity will deliver us. For the Christian the past is not lost. I once read an article by a cathedral canon who foresaw great joy to be had in heaven from the opportunity to meet long-dead figures who have been an inspiration to us in our earthly lives. The notion of being able to shake hands with Shakespeare and murmur congratulatory phrases of appreciation to Beethoven and Mozart certainly has its attractions. But as soon as you begin to picture the event difficulties arise.

For clearly the long line which would form before

Beethoven's residence or Shakespeare's would suggest a system of evaluation which is probably foreign to heaven. I do not mean to suggest that the long line for meeting Beethoven would be a cause of sadness and envy to the gifted composers who never got their works performed or gained any kind of recognition. But surely we feel that the afterlife which corrects the disparities of earthly experience between a wealthy Dives and a poverty-stricken Lazarus must also somehow correct the disparity of public recognition. Perhaps it even corrects the disparity of native talent, between the world-famous genius and the unknown aspirant.

There is a much-studied fourteenth century poem written in Middle English called *Pearl*. Its survival in manuscript form is one of the happiest accidents of English literary history. At the time of the dissolution of the monasteries, there were cultured people who rescued such literary treasures from destruction.

Pearl is an elegy. A father has lost his child, a baby girl of two. Visiting her grave in his grief, he falls asleep and sees a vision. At the other side of a river his lost daughter appears transfigured. She is wise now and instructs her father in how to dispel his grief and to rejoice in her present state in heaven. He calls her his Pearl, though the more usual version of the name was Marguerite or Margaret. But the pearl is the symbol of salvation:

> The kingdom of heaven is like unto a merchant man, seeking goodly pearls: Who, when he had found one pearl of great price, went and sold all that he had, and bought it. (Mt 13:45-46)

Interestingly enough, the girl wears a pearl on her breast, the token of her betrothal to the Lamb. She is crowned with a coronet of pearls, and her white robes are decked with pearls. Far from being lost, she assures her father that his pearl is preserved in a strong and comely chest. He was wrong to call fate a thief for bereaving him of her. Indeed, she is now the bride of the Lamb, Queen of Heaven. The father is astounded to hear this claim. Surely, the Virgin Mary is the Queen of Heaven. As for Pearl herself, she did not reach the age of two. She did not know a word of the Lord's Prayer or the Creed. She had not even begun to learn consciously how to please God or to pray to him.

Abundance in Heaven

Pearl replies by recalling our Lord's parable of the vineyard (Mt 20:1-10). The householder hires laborers early in the morning to work in the vineyard, agreeing to pay them a penny a day. He adds to their number throughout the day. When the day's work is done and the men are to be paid, the householder angers those who have toiled all day by putting them on an equality with the latecomers.

Yet no agreement has been broken. The householder has been generous to those he set to work late in the day. Why should generosity provoke resentment? "Is thine eye evil because I am good?" It is interesting to find in this medieval poem emphasis laid so strongly on the egalitarianism of heaven. Christ's declaration "So the last shall be first, and the first last" (Mt 20:16) is yet another instance of that over-turning of relative earthly evaluations which was so painfully represented in the story of Dives and Lazarus.

The medieval poem brings out two illuminating aspects of this egalitarianism. The one is the lesson that we are saved by grace and not by merit, and that grace equalizes all. The other is a lesson which at first taxes the father's understanding. Pearl announces that she is the Lamb's chosen Bride and crowned Queen of Heaven, and immediately the father begins to talk in terms of earthly competitiveness. The Virgin Mary is the Queen of Heaven, he says. "Who can take from her that crown unless she excels her in some quality?" The question is meaningless to a dweller in heaven. It is a property of the Court of Heaven of the living God, says Pearl, that each person who comes there is king or queen of the whole without depriving anyone of anything. This is what membership of the body of Christ means.

I have dealt with this aspect of heaven in my book, *Words Made Flesh* (published in the United Kingdom as *The Marks of the Maker* by Kingsway Publications in Eastbourne, 1987). In conceiving of the individual's salvation there is a good deal in the New Testament about "the crown of life, which the Lord hath promised to them that love him" (Jas 1:12). In earthly terms the crown is the symbol of unique sovereignty or unique victory. There is one crowned sovereign to a kingdom and the general distribution of crowns would make a mockery of monarchy. There is one laurel wreath or crown for the victor in the games, and the general distribution of the symbols of victory would make a mockery of the competition. Picture a cosmic Olympic Games in which all competitors in all events come away with gold medals. Yet that seems to be what is promised in heaven. "Be thou faithful unto death, and I will give thee a crown of life" (Rv 2:10).

Heavenly triumph, then, differs from all kinds of earthly triumph. The majesty of the earthly king denotes his uniqueness in relation to his millions of subjects. The glory of the earthly victor in the games denotes his own uniqueness in relation to those he immediately defeated and those many more who never got past the primary trials for the event. In heaven there is majesty without dominion over anyone. There is glory without superiority to anyone. There is rule without subjection, victory without defeat. The poet of *Pearl* handles this theme neatly.

The sequence of argument might have been very different. The father might have expressed his astonishment at his daughter's magnificently royal robes and she might have replied: "But that's nothing. It's not in the least out of the ordinary here. We're all like this in heaven." For on earth what is the property of everyone is scarcely worth remarking upon. It is superiority to the common run of things, and difference from the common run of things that matters on earth. But

Pearl rejoices just as exultantly in her dignity and status as she would if she were the sole Bride of the Lamb, the sole Queen of Heaven. Indeed she rejoices *the more* in her status for the fact that it is shared. "Each is glad for what the other has." The multiplication is an enrichment of the glory.

We are here concerned with various aspects of a single theme. The theme is that of loss, or deprivation, an experience peculiar to life in time, from which life in heaven will deliver us. On earth if you are lucky enough to own a particularly beautiful house with a garden sloping down to a river and a view of rolling downs beyond, your possession of this valued prize is matched by everyone else's deprivation of it. Some of your acquaintances may have even more beautiful houses. They may be even more beautifully situated. But others have nothing to compare with your home and they envy you.

On earth if some gifted young person acquires the stunning skills of a virtuoso violinist, a mark of his or her achievement is its rarity. As an audience of some thousands sits rapt in silence while the virtuoso plays the Tchaikovsky violin concerto, an aspect of their awe and even of their delight is the fact that none of them has anything like the amazing dexterity of hand and brain which makes possible these seemingly magical effects. From none of those listening is the thought not present at some point during the performance, what a wonderful gift! This combination of musical understanding, physical agility, tonal sensitivity, and emotional range! How remote it is from anything I could myself do with a musical instrument! How marvelous and how enviable he or she is!

An aspect of the experience, then, is that the violinist has something which the numerous members of the audience lack. Their deprivation highlights the wonder of the violinist's possession. You might translate the matter into crude market terms and say that the issue is simply one of supply and demand. Two or three thousand people want to hear the Tchaikovsky violin concerto played, and there is only one person in the concert hall who can play it.

The value of rarity arises from the discrepancy between the one who has a treasure and the many who lack it. It is difficult for us to think of an existence where all that is good or beautiful or wonderful about a possession could be totally disentangled from its rarity. It is difficult, in other words, to think of possession of such talent without its converse, deprivation. Yet the poet of *Pearl* insists that in heaven such is the case, and he makes use of our Lord's parable of the vineyard to establish the point.

I do not wish to suggest that all the citizens of heaven will be able to play the violin like Kreisler, to play the piano like Liszt, to paint like Michaelangelo, and to write plays like Shakespeare. The notion of a heaven wholly populated by brilliant executors of any art to which they might turn their hands is too fanciful. But somehow heaven must resolve the problem implicitly tackled by the poet of *Pearl*. What a person has cannot there depend on what other people lack, just as what a person achieves cannot there depend on what others fail to achieve. As a criterion of value, rarity must surely be unknown in heaven.

Indeed, it seems to follow from our Lord's story of Dives and Lazarus that if any contrast is to be drawn between the delights of what we have loosely called possession and the emptiness of deprivation, then it must be drawn between heaven and hell. If envy can obtain in eternity, it can only be the envy of a Dives for a Lazarus, of hell for heaven. The truth is that we have to think of heaven—if we trouble to brood on the matter at all—as a place where variety and multiplicity can exist without anywhere any sense of lack or deficiency. There will be neither motive nor reason for envying what another has or can do. Delight in what others can do will be as natural as delight in what we can do ourselves. The image which the poet puts into Pearl's mouth in explaining this to her father is the biblical one:

We are all members of Jesus Christ. Hand and arm and leg and trunk all serve the body they belong to: and every

Christian soul is a limb of the Lord. The head doesn't feel resentful or spiteful if there is a bracelet on an arm or a ring on a finger.

If heaven is to put an end to any possible sense of lack or deprivation, then surely heaven must abound with the most lavish provisions of talent and beauty, of character and insight. So many people on earth want so much that they lack. If it is worth having, are they going to be fully satisfied in heaven? Here we have to be careful not to mesmerize ourselves with overpowering concepts. So far as figures and quantities are concerned, heaven cannot be conceived in terms of earthly dimensions. Indeed our Lord warned us of the adjustment of our scales of measurement which we have to make in thinking of heaven:

> The kingdom of heaven is like to a grain of mustard seed, which a man took, and sowed in his field: Which indeed is the least of all seeds: but when it is grown, it is the greatest among herbs, and becometh a tree, so that the birds of the air come and lodge in the branches thereof. (Mt 13:31-32)

The smallest grain of seed becomes a tree that birds can nest in. The emphasis is purely on heaven's magnitude. For in moving from thoughts of earth to thoughts of heaven, we have to visualize an expansion of the kind that converts a seed into a tree. And, of course, our Lord gave concrete expression to this aspect of heaven as a place of abundance beyond earthly dreams when he took the five loaves and the two small fishes and transformed them into a meal for five thousand people.

The gravest earthly deprivation which life in heaven will correct is the loss of our loved ones. For the Christian the past which is irrecoverable on earth is recoverable in heaven. It may be argued that of all the things built into earthly life by the divine Creator, this is what most powerfully argues that life in time is not the be-all and end-all. The Creator has implanted in the human heart a deep resistance to the idea that when your wife or your mother, your husband or your father dies, that is the end of them.

To visit and tend graves, to mark anniversaries of death by memorial addresses to the deceased in the personal columns of newspapers, indicates a conviction that their personalities do not evaporate into thin air as their corpses rot in the soil. The firm conviction of many a widow or widower, that on their own death they will rejoin their partner, testifies to the same truth. Any notion of heaven which did not in this respect repair the ravages of time would be totally unacceptable.

Our Lord's promise is of everlasting life, and it would be quite illogical to take this as meaning that a man takes up in heaven exactly where he left off on earth. The idea that an eighty-year-old invalid who dies of a stroke will have to be wheeled into heaven in a wheelchair is clearly absurd. If the baby who dies before she can speak cannot remain in heaven forever a dumb infant, neither can the worn old man remain forever there a doddering senior citizen.

To be released from time is to be released from the ravages of time and from the tyranny of time. The ravages of time are all those marks of physical and mental deterioration which the passing decades inflict on us. The tyranny of time is that rigidity of clock and calendar which, by isolating us in the present moment, locks us away from the experience and responsiveness which we enjoyed twenty years ago or which we shall enjoy twenty years hence. Surely, if the escape from time's dominion means anything at all, it means that we are enabled to enjoy at one and the same time the vigor and freshness of youth and the wisdom and stability of age. It means that achievement need not be paid for by decay. It means that profundity need not be divorced from hope.

I just opened the *Oxford Companion to Music*. On one page there are photographs of Tchaikovsky at the age of twenty-three, thirty-seven, and fifty-three. The last represents the year of his death. Nothing could more eloquently display the costliness of human progress through time. The first photograph is a study of fresh-faced determination. There may be a hint of premature brooding gravity about the eyes, but the clean-cut features and the folded arms speak of a personality more than equal to cope with what life may throw up. The second photograph speaks to me of nothing so much as bewilderment. Perhaps the pince-nez spectacles have something to do with an expression which manages to be faintly quizzical and strangely pained at the same time. The third photograph has a tragic grandeur in its expression of agony wrestled with and unresolved.

Yet this was the man who had to his credit not only the brooding solemnities of the Pathetique Symphony but also the incredibly rich treasury of spontaneous melody, irresistible rhythm, and luscious orchestration of the Nutcracker ballet. The passage of time which allowed this man to add immeasurable wealth to the concert programs of the next century reduced him personally, it appears, to a figure of melancholy desolation. We cannot superimpose on the composer who had fashioned so much beauty the physical persona of the young man of twenty-three. But if Tchaikovsky is in heaven, it cannot be the Tchaikovsky of fifty-three, grievously bowed down with the weight of life's burden.

Not many of us have either the creativity of a Tchaikovsky or the neurotic temperament of a Tchaikovsky. But any of us who has reached the age of fifty or beyond might assemble a series of photographs of ourselves or our contemporary loved ones and might be moved to wish that somehow we could extract what is good from each phase of life and lose what is bad. We might wish that we could keep the valuable experience or perhaps the wisdom that the decades have brought us and slough off all the damaging effects of the passage of time. We desire to gather in from the past and the present to make a completion of all that is good. We are like the householder mentioned by our Lord when he spoke of the continuing relevance of the old Law to the newly regenerate. "Therefore every scribe which is instructed unto the kingdom of heaven is like unto a man that is a householder, which bringeth forth out of his treasure things new and old" (Mt 13:52).

Perfection in Heaven

We rightly want to have the best of things new and old, and this is only one aspect of our need to transcend time's limitations. For there is a fragmentary quality about even the finest experiences in our life in time. We want to pull the fragments together: that tingling sensitivity to a beautiful sunset or a beautiful girl which coursed through our veins in our teens. Why cannot we have it alongside that poise and self-assurance which we attained only in our late thirties? Why cannot we have it alongside our understanding of its connection with a dozen other awakenings to the mystery of the created order which we arrived at only in our forties?

It is in fragmentary glimpses that the joys of the kingdom are flashed before our faces on our earthly pilgrimage. We all have our stores of memories that keep their power to blind us with the dazzle of the wonder and beauty they revealed. When you first took a hand that is now cold in the grave—when you first looked into eyes that imprinted their gaze forever on your mind—when you first caught sight of that remote village nestling in the elbow of a valley, all white and green in the sun—when you first saw your wife with your baby in her arms—when a lyric of Byron's first throbbed through your brain in school days—when Toscanini revitalized the fabric of a Beethoven symphony—when Maria Callas released flooding waves of emotion upon a few syllables, "Alfin son tua," in Donizetti's *Lucia di Lammermoor*: we all have our store of such particular memories. If we wanted a single adjective to characterize what was common to them all, we should say quite naturally, quite unaffectedly, "It was heavenly."

We very often add those other words and say "It was heavenly while it lasted." This most natural of expressions carries immense implications. To say "It was heavenly" of any experience is to imply that you have been briefly lifted above the humdrum level of experience proper to earthly life and given a glimpse, or rather a taste, of life at a level of wonder and delight which is proper to heaven. Our literature and our conversation have long been littered with usages of the words *heaven* and *heavenly* as descriptive of life's most joyful experiences.

When Wordsworth wanted to say, not just how wonderful, but how overwhelmingly wonderful it was to be a young man when the French Revolution broke out, he said:

Bliss was it in that dawn to be alive,
But to be young was very heaven! (*The Prelude*)

It was bliss to be alive at such a historic moment of human liberation. But to be young too—how can he express an intensity of delight beyond the raptures which the word bliss conjures up? There is only one possible expression equal to the height of extreme ecstasy. It was very heavenly. When Milton wanted to convey how the music of choir and organ could transfix him with its magnificence, he spoke of a sweetness that could dissolve him "into ecstasies." But the climactic expression of overpowering wonder was that it could "bring all Heaven before mine eyes" (*Il Penseroso*).

Now this use of language common to the poet and to the man in the street is indeed exactly representative of the relationship between heaven and earth in one respect. The heavenly does impinge on the earthly. That is what we should expect. The earth was divinely created. It must be expected to show the Maker's hand at work. The earth was divinely visited. It was a fit environment for God in his humanity to dwell in.

But God in Jesus Christ did not settle down here to be six feet of human flesh for the rest of time, walking earth's streets and making it inescapable for the human mind to come to terms with him. He settled here only in the body of his church which can never be so purely and obviously the vehicle of his divine presence that all are compelled to acknowledge it.

I am trying to establish two points. The first is that a divinely created and divinely visited world will naturally bear the marks of its Creator and in that way offer evidence of the glory in which he dwells. The second point is that evidence of the glory must necessarily be conveyed in fragmentary glimpses. Otherwise, human freedom to respond to God or not respond to God would be lost. The fragmentation of the heavenly as it impinges on the earthly is the price of human freedom. After all, even the divine incarnation of God in Christ provided us with but a fragmentary earthly contact of heaven with earth, since Christ came at a particular point in history into a particular locality to make contact with a particular group of people.

The incarnation itself is thus but a fragmented incursion of divinity upon the human scene. You might say that God submitted himself to that fragmentation of the heavenly which is all that can be glimpsed on earth. And the climax of that fragmentary incursion into human affairs was the fragmentation of the Redeemer himself, the body broken on the cross.

As his body was broken on the cross, so too the Christian body—the church—has been fragmented through history. I sometimes think that we worry too much about this external fragmentation of the Christian body. Since all things earthly, insofar as they make contact with or reveal the heavenly, can do so only in a fragmentary way it is not surprising that the church is thus fragmented.

But this is a digression from our immediate concern. On earth the contacts with the heavenly and the glimpses of the heavenly have a fragmentary character which affects our human response in two ways.

In the first place, because the glimpses and tastes of the heavenly are brief and fleeting, we men and women can dismiss them from our minds as delusive, imaginary, unreliable, and not to be seriously taken into account in defining the nature of our human pilgrimage. In short, because they are fragmentary we can ignore them as evidence of the divine Creator's hand and as evidence of a life beyond time where there is indeed glory and wonder. In the second place, however, the fragmentariness of human glimpses and tastes of the heavenly can have quite the opposite effect on men and women. The glimpses stir the appetite for a fuller entry into the glory so tantalizingly experienced. The fragment makes us hungry for the whole.

The Victorian poet Elizabeth Barrett Browning put the situation very neatly in her narrative poem *Aurora Leigh*:

> Earth's crammed with heaven,
> And every common bush afire with God:
> But only he who sees, takes off his shoes;
> The rest sit round it, and pluck blackberries . . .

We may sit around plucking blackberries, deriving our food and pleasure from the things God has made in total thoughtlessness. Or we may be alert to the burning presence of God in creation and metaphorically remove our shoes in recognition of, and reverence for, the way he is revealed in his works.

Earthly experiences of many kinds give us a fleeting taste of what will be the joys hereafter. "The kingdom of God is within you," our Lord declared (Lk 17:21). There are those Christians for whom silent meditation away from all earthly interests and concerns can bring an experience of release from all the fettering limitations of life in time. Men and women with a high degree of spirituality tell us how they withdraw in contemplation. It is withdrawal from conscious participation in the world of hours and minutes, of wanting and planning, of coming and going. In this way they can experience release from all life's pressures and compulsions.

They enter into a state of stillness. The self is emptied of normal preoccupations. It is opened in surrender to the presence of God. And it is filled with a tranquillity unattainable by any other human route: "the peace which passeth understanding." Here, in the mystic's total self-opening to the divine

indwelling, is an ecstasy of total release from all the wanting
and longing, the claiming and demanding, which preoccupy
our egos in the world.

Now some who have experienced this kind of spiritual
ecstasy have felt a kind of letdown in the return to normal
consciousness of the world around them. Emily Brontë wrote
a poem entitled "The Prisoner" in which an experience of
mystical escape is described in rapturous images. The invisible dawns, outward sense is gone, and "inward essence
feels." It is as though the soul's wings are suddenly freed so
that it can fly to its true home and harbor. But the rebound is
painful indeed:

> O dreadful is the check—intense the agony—
> When the ear begins to hear, and the eye begins to see;
> When the pulse begins to throb—the brain to think again—
> The soul to feel the flesh, and the flesh to feel the chain.

These words are put into the mouth of a prisoner, declaring
to the tyrants who have confined him that his spirit is
unconquerable and has its own resources. No doubt they
reflect the poet's own experience of the contrast between the
mystical reception of the divine vision and some of the
harrowing realities of daily life. "I see heaven's glories shine,"
Emily Brontë wrote later in her last poem as a dying
consumptive:

> Though earth and man were gone,
> And suns and universe cease to be,
> And Thou were left alone,
> Every existence would exist in thee. (*No Coward Soul Is Mine*)

The contrast between the mystical ecstasy and the humdrum
realities of daily life is of course unnaturally exaggerated if the
mystic is locked in a dungeon or dying of consumption. But the
contrast highlights the fact that this mode of entry into
communion with the divine is achieved by turning the back on

the normal responses of the mind and the senses to the character of life in time. For this reason the process of disciplined self-emptying of all desire, attachment, and longing as a route to mystical rapture has been called the Way of Negation. It is so called because the back is turned on the created world and the self is separated from responsiveness to it.

By contrast what has been called the Way of Affirmation is the route to delight in God's presence, in his wonder and his power, which is opened up by our sensitive response to the world he has made and the creatures he has made. We may sit round the bush and pluck blackberries. We may see the bush of blackberries as afire with God and remove our shoes. The poet exaggerates the contrast, you may say. After all, God made the blackberries to be eaten, and there would seem to be no good reason why we should not both enjoy the fruit and duly praise the Maker for the bush.

But clearly the poet is speaking of that Affirmative Way into the divine presence, found not by turning our back on the things of earth, in this case the bush, but by responding to what they can convey of God's touch upon creation. We meet our Lord in his creation and delight in the created order of things.

We have all at some point of our lives spoken of this or that experience as being heavenly. But we have not always paused to reflect what its heavenliness had to teach us, or indeed paused to respond graciously and thankfully to the Giver for his gift. It was music which brought all heaven before Milton's eyes. It was the beauty of natural scenery which gave Wordsworth his entry into mystical bliss. It was having his beloved before him on horseback which caused Browning's lover in *The Last Ride Together* to argue that perhaps after all heaven might be no more than an immortalization of present bliss:

> What if we still ride on, we two,
> With life for ever old yet new,
> Changed not in kind but in degree,
> The instant made eternity.

Earthly life is littered with glimpses of heaven and foretastes of heaven. It is also, as we have seen, littered with glimpses of hell and foretastes of hell. We have seen too that life in the flesh shields and shelters us from what would be the unbearable ecstasy or the unbearable agony of closer acquaintance here and now with the heavenly or the hellish. For among the characteristics of heaven which must distinguish its life from the life of earth, there is one which we have not yet mentioned.

We have spoken of that permanence and stability of the heavenly which will deliver us from everything which makes earthly life ephemeral and insecure. We have spoken of how all the possibilities of deprivation and loss which mar earth's finest experiences will be unknown in heaven. We have observed how triumph and victory will be separated in heaven from their earthly counterparts, failure and defeat. We have dwelt on the sheer abundance of heavenly provisions. We have seen how what is partial and fragmentary in earthly delights and achievements will be merged in experiences of wholeness and fullness inconceivable here below.

There must be added to this catalog of heaven's fulfillments a characteristic of heavenly life which might be called its *intensity* or its *concentration*. It seems to be indicated in our Lord's brief declaration, "The kingdom of heaven is like unto leaven, which a woman took, and hid in three measures of meal, till the whole was leavened" (Mt 13:33). If the stability of things heavenly contrasts with the fleetingness of the earthly, and if the fullness of things heavenly contrasts with the fragmentariness of the earthly, then the sheer intensity of things heavenly contrasts with the diffuseness of things earthly. The heavenly impinges on the earthly only fitfully and fragmentarily. It also impinges on the earthly in an attenuated form. Neither the glory nor the beauty of heaven, neither the love nor the joy of heaven, can be tasted without dilution by creatures of flesh and blood. That glory and that beauty, that love and that joy, are diffused through the substance of earthly experience to vivify and transfigure it as the yeast permeates the coarse measures of meal.

In our day we perhaps scarcely need imagery of yeast and bread to suggest the concentration of vitality in a small measure which can infuse a vastly larger substance. Nor perhaps do we need imagery of seed and tree to suggest the potentiality of magnitude packed into a minute volume. For understanding of the nuclear construction of the physical world has given us an appreciation of how gigantically explosive powers can be locked within an infinitesimal atom. We ought not to have difficulty in appreciating that rapturous and exultant as our most ecstatic moments on earth may be, they scarcely hint at that release of expansive delight which floods and drenches the inhabitants of heaven.

Great poets have sometimes spoken of rapturous moments in the experience of love of beauty which have seemed to represent such a climactic immersion in delight that death itself, rather than a return to mundane reality, would be an appropriate termination of bliss. When Othello receives his bride Desdemona safely into his arms in Cyprus after their perilous voyage, he voices a momentary bliss which is to be rarely his:

> If it were now to die
> 'Twere now to be most happy, for I fear
> My soul hath her content so absolute,
> That not another comfort like to this
> Succeeds in unknown fate. (*Othello*)

Such is the present bliss, so absolute the soul's contentment, that there can never possibly be anything in life to compare with it. Therefore to die at this moment would be to die at the peak of happiness.

The notion of a bliss so intense that even long years of life will be by comparison trivial, wasteful, and rather sad, is one that emerges from the experience of some mystics. The inconceivable intensity of joy and love, beauty and glory, which appertain to life in heaven is a sure measure of what salvation means. The converse intensity of misery in its loss is of course what damnation means. Such is the reality of heaven and hell.

SIX

Hope of Heaven

Is it a Selfish Dream?

There can be no doubt from our Lord's own words that the kingdom of heaven is to be the focus of the Christian's hopes and strivings. Yet when we try to picture heavenly life, as we have just been doing, a niggling doubt intrudes at the back of the mind. If we conceive of the best and most wonderful of earthly experiences transfigured and immortalized in a time-less life where there can be neither decay nor privation, are we not fixing our minds on what is supremely satisfying to the self? Does not this raise questions for the sensitive conscience? There is an old Latin hymn, once believed to have been the work of Francis Xavier, the great Jesuit missionary, which has been translated in our modern hymn books:

My God, I love thee; not because
   I hope for heaven thereby,
Nor yet because who love thee not
   Are lost eternally. (*O Deus ego amo te*; translated by E. Caswall)

The poet seems to recognize an element of selfishness in loving God out of hope of heaven and fear of hell. He goes on to recount the sufferings Christ endured on the cross. They were endured "all for me." Is there not enough reason here for loving Christ without reference to the desire to win heaven and escape hell? The basis of the Christian's response to Christ is not the hope of reward. It is a matter of returning love for love.

There has been a tendency in the past to mock Christians by asserting that their worship and their attempts to be good are a way of earning a passage to heaven and escaping damnation. As such, all Christian effort can be mocked as self-centered. There are of course hymns which look to heaven as the faithful pilgrim's reward when life is over. But if love of God—or even the will to love God—is the basis of the Christian's persistence in the faith, then it would be misleading to describe as selfish the hope of entering into the kingdom God has called us to.

When two people in love plan to marry and look forward to the wedding with passionate longing, you would not denigrate their hope as selfish. Perhaps they look forward to a happiness beyond their wildest dreams. Perhaps they picture the bliss of the coming honeymoon and the subsequent weeks and years of life in each other's company as a prospect of continuing ecstasy. You might accuse them of being starry-eyed, but you would not charge them with selfishness. Each wants what the other wants. If there is any truth in the gospel at all, then God wants his creatures with him in heaven.

Now you may say to yourself: "Ah yes, God may love me as a young man loves his bride-to-be. But alas, I cannot pretend to feel for him any such overpowering passion. I know I ought to love him as a bride loves a bridegroom. But, if I am honest, that is quite beyond me."

Then let us pursue the analogy of the earthly lovers a little further. Suppose one of them, say the bride-to-be, is not quite so sure as her future partner that she can indeed match his love with her love. Suppose she has qualms. "He seems to adore me. He thinks I'm more wonderful and beautiful than I really am. I can't live up to it. I should not go to the altar with him unless I can answer his overwhelming love with matching devotion."

I do not cite such an instance in order to advise a young girl to rush into marriage with doubts in her mind about the wisdom of doing so. But if there *were* a bride-to-be thinking like that and she determined to go through with the wedding nevertheless, you could not call her selfish. Yes, you might call her imprudent or rash. You might call her unwisely unselfish or even heroically unselfish. But you could not call her behavior selfish.

God's love for us is prior to any love we may have for him. "Ye have not chosen me, but I have chosen you," our Lord said to his disciples (Jn 15:16). And the apostle John declared, "Herein is love, not that we loved God, but that he loved us, and sent his Son to be the propitiation for our sins" (1 Jn 4:10). Illogical as it may seem to us, God actually *wants* us in his kingdom. And it is not a matter of wanting more recruits as the ambitious party leader wants to add ever more and more names to his list of supporters.

Disproportionate as it may seem to us, God actually wants us for ourselves, for what we are. We may be as incapable of feeling love for God as we are of understanding why he should bother to love us. But if we go forward in the Christian life in faith, listening to the promise held out of the kingdom of heaven, though we may be accused by the world of rashness, we cannot be charged with selfishness. In wanting heaven, we want for ourselves what God wants for us.

If we want something for ourselves primarily because God wants it for us, we are displaying something which in human beings must always perhaps be there prior to love of God, that is respect for God. Respect is a cold word. A better word might be honor. The apostle John tells us that the Father has "committed all judgment unto the Son: That all men should honor the Son, even as they honor the Father. He that honoreth not the Son honoreth not the Father which hath sent him" (Jn 5:22-23).

We certainly owe respect to the God who created us. And even in purely human terms if someone sacrifices his life for us, we have a duty to respect him for the rest of our days. From that duty of respect to our Creator and our Redeemer certain obligations follow before ever there is a mention of answering love with love. The obligations involve adjusting ourselves to the prescriptions and to the wishes of the one to whom we are in debt for our very existence.

We have established that there is nothing intrinsically selfish in hoping for heaven. But that does not mean that fixing one's gaze on future bliss may not take on a selfish character. Indeed, when we devoted a chapter to imagining what heavenly life must be like and—in particular—how it must transcend in joy and wonder the most rapturous experiences of life in time, we were surely running a great risk. Perhaps all pictures of heavenly life conceived by earthbound imaginations will focus on the wrong things.

We cannot project images of heavenly feasting without wondering whether, after all, eternal life can possibly need to be sustained by anything approximate to physical nourishment. We think of the most lavish of earthly banquets as taking their toll in indigestion. We suspect that nothing corresponding to the human digestive system can properly be immortalized in an eternal kingdom. We conclude that projecting earthly delights onto an eternal plane may well stem from an unwillingness to loosen the grip on things worldly which we ought to rise above. We are tempted to feel superior because we do not picture a Muslim Paradise in which we shall be voluptuously entertained by luscious houris or beautiful maidens.

Do not mistake the drift of this argument. It would be quite wrong to suggest that all who have pictured heaven in terms of earthly delights transfigured and eternalized have been guilty of misrepresentation. God gave us our earthly environment. God gave us our human minds to respond to it and interpret it. If he sets a kingdom of heaven before us as our true and proper final home and urges us to accept it as a place of everlasting joy, then he can scarcely rebuke us if we turn our minds to explore its delights in advance.

Or can he? Is there a catch here? After all, we have been

urged to set our hearts on things above and not on things here below.

> Lay not up for yourselves treasures upon earth, where moth and rust doth corrupt, and where thieves break through and steal: But lay up for yourselves treasures in heaven, where neither moth nor rust doth corrupt, and where thieves do not break through nor steal: For where your treasure is, there will your heart be also. (Mt 6:19-21)

If we respond to this advice by taking the most enjoyable of earthly experiences and saying "These will be ours in heaven without interruption or alloy," are we not hoarding up our earthly treasures, packing them into a box, wrapping it up, addressing it to ourselves, to await collection by the addressee at the heavenly post office after our safe arrival?

In the long run, there is probably only one way of escape from the dangers of dressing up worldly things in celestial vesture and calling it our dream of heaven. The escape is to stop thinking about ourselves enjoying this or that and to start thinking about God instead. Does this mean that the substance of the previous chapter was riddled with worldliness and selfishness? I do not think so. If we are asked for a humanly devised forecast of heavenly bliss, all we can do is to exercise our minds and think in terms of transfigured earthly experience.

But having done so, it is time to call a halt. It is time to recognize that an earthly dream is one thing and heavenly reality quite another thing. An earthly dream serves as a nudge toward seeking a happiness and fulfillment that earth can never supply. And that may be useful enough. But to fasten hope and longing, ambition and aspiration, on the concrete imagery of this world, however idealized, has in it at least the seeds of selfishness and possessiveness. All earthly dreams of heaven are surely things to be toyed with, briefly relished, and then cast aside.

C.S. Lewis, in his paper *Christianity and Literature,* draws attention to the way in which Dante pictures Pope Gregory I arriving in heaven. He quickly discovers that his carefully worked-out theory of the angelic hierarchies was all wrong. He is vastly amused. One might suggest that if we were to arrive in heaven and discover that some of our ideas in the previous chapter were not utterly irrelevant, were not even totally wide of the mark, but actually sometimes hit the bullseye, then we should surely have even greater cause for laughter.

The Sight of God

There is a paradox here which puts Christians in a dilemma when their thoughts turn to heaven. In the first place, it is right to regard earthly joys as providing a foretaste of heaven. Indeed, the kingdom of heaven is within us already if we are trying to be faithful Christians. In the second place, the essence of heavenly bliss, we are told, lies in an unimpeded relationship to God which is impossible on earth. Insofar as we try to picture heaven in terms of perfected human delights, we tend to project into heavenly life a self-centeredness inappropriate to it. Insofar as we try to picture heaven in terms of a perfected relationship to God—revealed and known as he can never be revealed and known to us on earth—our human understanding falters. Our thinking quickly evaporates into abstractions.

Nevertheless, there have been Christians whose mental grasp upon heaven has been such that the highest earthly delights have seemed to be, not a basis for yearning for heaven, but a hindrance to longing for God. Let me take as an example a little known Christian, Ann Griffiths, born in Wales in 1776 into a farming family. For two-thirds of her short life she and her family were faithful members of the Anglican church in Wales. They were then caught up by the tide of the Methodist revival, which provided Ann with a spiritual home. Religion apart, there is little to say about the course of life of a girl who lost her mother when she was eighteen and thereafter kept house for her father and brothers. She herself married in 1804, only to die a year later after giving birth to a daughter.

Ann was deeply stirred by a rare inner vision, and her religious raptures inspired her to the composition of hymns in her native Welsh. Even in an English translation, the vigor and richness of Ann's imaginative gifts are striking. The theme of longing for the heavenly home, of eagerness to escape earth's idols, of desire to "come to the King's table," is powerfully voiced. Ann imagines how wonderful it will be to come out of the fiery furnace and "be fine gold at last." By comparison the continuing earthly struggle against evil is wearisome and harassing. An overwhelmingly dominant love for Christ makes all earthly attachments seem trivial:

> Earth cannot, with all its trinkets,
>   Slake my longings at this hour;
> They were captured, they were widened
>   When my Jesus showed his power.
> None but he can now content me,
>   He, the Incomprehensible;
> O to gaze upon his Person,
>   God in man made visible.

(*Homage to Ann Griffiths*, hymns by Ann Griffiths translated by H.A. Hodges, Penarth, United Kingdom: Church in Wales Publications, 1976; see p. 53.)

The case of Ann Griffiths is cited because she seems to have been one of those people of rare sanctity whose faith enables them to come to terms with death. She wrote thus of her own death:

Dear Sister, I can say that what cheers me more than anything in these days is this—not death in itself, but the great gain that is to be got through it. To be able to leave behind every inclination that goes against the will of God, to leave behind every ability to dishonour the Law of God. (*op. cit.*, p. 20)

Ann's hope of heaven is the hope of at last being adjusted in all her ways to what God wills for her. Her sentences are at once a great stimulus and a great consolation. They are a stimulus in the sense that they provide an inspiring model. The Christian learns to see death as something from which "a great gain" is to be derived. And the sentences are a consolation to us because what Ann Griffiths *wants* to get away from is "every inclination that goes against the will of God." So even the poet of the rapturous longings for Christ's presence concedes that she still has to deal with inclinations that go against God's will.

There is hope for us all then. We know all about inclinations that go against God's will. Inclinations is a key word. If we feel an inclination to go against God's will, then with a part of ourselves we *want* to go against God's will. Yes, you will say, but there is another part of ourselves which does not want to go against God's will. It wants to obey God's will in all things.

Plainly there are two levels of wanting. I want to stay in bed on a Sunday morning. I *want* to want to get up and go to church. I want success and wealth. I *want* to want to serve God in humility and self-discipline. I want continuing health and vigor, life and joy on God's earth. I *want* to want the bliss of heaven. Or is that not too strong? Is it not safer to say: I'm afraid I *ought* to want the bliss of heaven?

This involvement of the Christian in the duplicities of life in time is inescapable. And when a writer begins to write about heaven he will have to try to sidestep them. For the writer has been instructed that the summit of heavenly joy lies in the beatific vision, the unimaginable privilege and bliss of lifting the eyelids in the presence of the Creator of all things who dwells forever in light and glory. The writer has been so instructed, and so he must surely believe. But can he, sitting in his chair, pen in hand, between breakfast and lunch, earnestly and honestly *want* to be whisked away from his home, his loved ones, the snow-covered mountaintop he can see through the study window—to be whisked summarily away and deposited before the awful throne of God?

Of course not. You and I were given our humanity. We did not devise or even choose its advantages or its limitations. No doubt the beatific vision is the glory and delight of souls in heaven. But we are not in heaven. We are on earth. There is no Christian obligation to count as nothing the joys and loves of the life we have been given here below. The Christ who told us to set our hearts on things above did not hesitate to heal earthly infirmities to render earthly life more enjoyable. He did not hesitate to join in a wedding feast. He did not even reject the pouring out of costly perfume upon his head by Mary Magdalene.

The incarnation proclaimed the potentialities of life in the flesh. The appearances of Christ after the resurrection, and the ascension of Christ in his human body define the way the human being can be transfigured. We are not in error then when we try to picture heavenly reality in terms of the transfiguration of the earthly. Christ's incarnation, resurrection, and ascension involved the annexation of the earthly by the heavenly.

It was while living on earth in a human body that the poet Ann Griffiths experienced the love of Christ so deeply and sensed the beauty of Christ so acutely that she yearned for the perfection of knowing him unbrokenly in heaven. Such longings as hers, therefore, evidence again the way the human heart and mind are stirred by fragmentary tastes of glory to conceive of unfragmented glory in heaven. However hard you strive to eliminate from dreams of heaven the hopes and longings that are bred of earthly stimulation through the senses and the emotions, you can never disinfect heaven of earth.

If you could, you would dehumanize yourself. And to try to dehumanize yourself is to devalue what the incarnate Christ for all time hallowed. As you cannot disinfect the heavenly of the earthly, so you cannot disinfect the divine of the human. It is too late. Christ annexed the human to the divine and carried it up to glory.

Nevertheless, as we have said, the danger in picturing a heaven in terms of earthly delights made perfect and permanent is that we may try to baptize our selfishness rather than conquer it. Christ's parables of the kingdom of heaven certainly build on common earthly experiences, but for the most part they are rather concerned to give teaching about who will get to heaven and who will not than to conjure up pictures of what heaven will be like.

The biblical visions of heaven make few concessions to what today we should call literary naturalism or literary realism. The four living creatures who emerge from the midst of cloud and fire before the prophet in Ezekiel have four faces each: one the face of a man, another of a lion, a third of an ox, and a fourth of an eagle. They have four wings each too. When Milton, in *Paradise Lost,* came to the point of having to describe how the Son rides out to do battle against the rebel angels under Satan and to drive them out of heaven, he used Ezekiel's vision. He pictured how four-winged "cherubic shapes" move the Son's chariot forward, their bodies and the wheels too set with jewelled eyes like stars, and flames racing between them. As in Ezekiel, the cherubic shapes have over their heads a crystal firmament which is itself a floor for the throne of sapphire on which the Son is seated.

This is far indeed from realistic portraiture in terms of life on earth. But Milton proves how powerful Ezekiel's symbolism is. For the Son rides out to battle enthroned on a mobile miniature universe. The Son's enthronement on this mobile heaven and earth symbolizes his lordship over the heavenly realm of angel and spirit, over the created universe of firmament and star, and over the living creatures, both man and beast.

The blend of the human, the animal, and the angelic in the shapes of the cherubic beings who draw the vehicle denotes a harmony and unity among the living creatures fashioned by God and subject to the Son. Even the fruitful blend of spirit and machinery in action has powerful significance in Milton's poem because it is by misuse of machinery that the rebel angels wreak havoc in battle.

Isaiah's celebrated vision of God in heaven is also heavily symbolic. The seraphim have six wings each, two to cover the face, two to cover the feet, and two with which to fly. As they hail God with their acclamation "Holy, Holy, Holy, is the LORD of hosts: the whole earth is full of his glory" (Is 6:3), the door-posts are shaken and the air is filled with smoke. To signify the purging of Isaiah's sins, a seraphim takes a burning coal from off the altar with a pair of tongs, flies to the prophet, and touches his mouth with it.

Milton used this passage too in picturing God the Father, "the Fountain of Light," invisible and inaccessible in the unfaceable and unsearchable brightness of his presence. When he draws around himself a shadowy cloud which veils his central blaze, then it becomes possible for the seraphim to approach. They cannot gaze with the naked eye even now, because around the fringes of the cloud the excessive brightness still dazzles and blinds. But they can approach with their eyes covered by the double folding of both wings.

The emphasis in such visions as these is on aspects of divine splendor which stagger the mind and stun the imagination of human beings. There is no attempt to suggest that life in heaven in proximity to God might be a congenial experience for a human being. The prophets dazzle us with flame and lightning, burning coals and rolling smoke. They conceive miraculously bodied beings and ransack the sky, the stars, and the catalog of precious stones for imagery of unearthly opulence and brilliance.

The environment sounds about as cozy as a magnified Palace of Versailles and about as reposeful as a perpetual firework display. This is no home of eternal peace to retire to after a long life of trouble and stress. Plainly, we are not intended to think of eternal rest as a matter of putting our feet up over the fireplace in a cozy country cottage with roses around the door. The prophets are determined to make us awestruck in God's presence. It is the awesomeness, the grandeur, and indeed the fearfulness of the divine majesty that the prophets unfold before our eyes.

The Vision of the Apostle John

The apostle John's vision of heaven in the Book of Revelation is in the same tradition. The apostle provides neither a Beginner's Guide to Heaven nor a travel agent's brochure, appetizingly advertising its tourist attractions. He did not set himself the task either of instructing us how to behave in heaven, or of urging us to make heaven the object of our earthly strivings. The apostle John was a visionary more concerned with how to convey what heaven means than to advise us how to get there or to help us find our niche on arrival.

A voice summons him like a trumpet call, and he sees God enthroned, blazing like a diamond or a topaz and haloed about by an emerald rainbow. Twenty-four white-robed elders sit around the throne, golden crowns on their heads. The throne itself emits thunder and lightning, while seven lamps burn before it. There is a crystal pavement like a sea of glass. Four living creatures around the throne—like a lion, a calf, a man, and a flying eagle—are covered with eyes. They are six-winged creatures, and they never cease to proclaim, "Holy, holy, holy, Lord God Almighty, which was and is and is to come" (Rv 4:8). Meanwhile, the four and twenty elders prostrate themselves before the throne proclaiming God's praise and glory, honor and power. And the slaughtered Lamb standing before the throne has seven horns and seven eyes.

It is only necessary to contrast John's image of the seven-horned, seven-eyed Lamb with the more common portrait of the gentle Jesus of the hymn book to cause us to reflect on John's purpose. The Jesus whose name sounds so sweetly in the believer's ear—soothes his sorrow, heals his wounds, and drives away his fear—is altogether more approachable than the Lamb, surrounded by the ten thousand times ten thousand voices of acclamation. This is the majestic Lamb of God who breaks the seals to send the four horsemen of the Apocalypse riding through history. Yet the tale of war and civil strife, of famine and pestilence, of persecution, and of wrathful cosmic upheaval unfolded by the breaking of the seals is not the last word.

For, with the breaking of the seventh seal, we have a vision of the countless host who have come out of great tribulation, "and have washed their robes, and made them white in the blood of the Lamb" (Rv 7:14). Indeed, at this point, the Lamb assumes the persona of the Good Shepherd who will feed them and "lead them unto living fountains of waters: and God shall wipe away all tears from their eyes" (Rv 7:17). This is one of those rare moments in the Book of Revelation when the vast fabric of imagery seems to crack momentarily with the resonance of everyday human emotion.

The apostle's climactic vision of the destruction of Babylon sees her as the harlot city, the home of all earth's abominations. Gorgeous in purple and scarlet, bedecked in sumptuous jewels, she is the great whore with whom the great and mighty and the wealthy and proud ones of the earth debauch themselves in sensuality and dissipation. The symbol of all worldliness which turns its back on God, the city is full of every kind of earthly treasure and abundance. The rich merchandise, the costly craftsmanship, the music, and the revelry in this seat of all affluence and self-indulgence are wiped off the face of the earth.

By contrast John is granted a vision of the New Jerusalem, the city given over to sanctity and obedience, "coming down from God out of heaven, prepared as a bride adorned for her husband" (Rv 21:2). The city is a spectacle of jewelled radiance and splendor. But the description does not set the heart thumping with nostalgic yearning for its one true home. The architecture is presented in terms of walls and gateways and foundation stones matching in number the twelve tribes of Israel.

For the rest, the city is geometrically conceived. Indeed, its measurements are described with such precision that the reader who has had any experience of mathematical examinations is likely to prepare himself mentally for some such culminating question as: If a man walks at three miles an hour, how long will it take him to walk around the city? But, of course, the sheer objectivity—the breathtaking objectivity of the apostle John's excursion into detail in respect of the city's dimensions—cuts away any vagueness and sentimentality from the mind. So too does his parallel inventory of precious stones employed in the construction of each section of the walls, gates, and streets. Whatever else we may know or not know about the New Jerusalem, there is one thing the apostle is determined to leave in our minds: The place has real substance. It has definite, exact measurements.

What is striking about the vision of the New Jerusalem is that it transfigures an urban and not a rural environment. "God and man made the town," the poet William Cowper wrote in *The Task*. And in all ages, hermits have sought to deepen their personal contact with God by seeking out peaceful spots in the countryside remote from city life. Poets have also found in nature the stimulus and inspiration for mystical glimpses of the eternal. Wordsworth gives an unnervingly forceful picture of rocky heights and warring winds, of black crags and "blasts of waterfalls," experienced on a walk through the Simplon Pass. Then he concludes his description by declaring of all these prospects:

> Tumult and peace, the darkness and the light—
> Were all like workings of one mind, the features
> Of the same face, blossoms upon one tree,
> Characters of the great Apocalypse,
> The types and symbols of Eternity,
> Of first, and last, and midst, and without end.
> (*The Simplon Pass*)

In the grandeur of the natural scene, then, Wordsworth sees the "workings of one mind" and "the features of the same face." The fabric of the natural world with all its variety embodies a single revelation. What this conveys to the poet's exultant mind is a glimpse of a splendor and stability beyond time. Such experiences show man in nature rather than man in society. They may be no less valid or hallowed for that. Solitaries in all ages have found joy and peace in communion with God. And even those not given to the solitary life have sensed God's presence behind the natural order with a sureness that is eloquent. Emily Brontë was no lover of the city. She was never happy when she was away from the moors around her Yorkshire home. Yet she could dispel all fear and doubt by declaring:

I see Heaven's glories shine
And faith shines equal, arming me from fear.
(No Coward Soul Is Mine)

We can scarcely bring ourselves today to conceive of heaven in terms of a typical twentieth century city. It is easier to identify our vast industrial cities with the apostle John's Babylon. Even those capitals which have architectural splendors at their center generally hide ugliness, vice, poverty, and dirt behind their noble facades. We may have visited cities whose former grandeur and beauty is finely preserved. No one who has walked about the streets of Florence today can fail to understand how Dante could make it an image of the divine city. But even Florence has its traffic jams nowadays. Standing on one of its street corners or bridges and dreaming yourself into the New Jerusalem would be a difficult task indeed. The expressways, the subways, and the towering steel and glass skyscrapers of the modern city cannot readily be transmuted into images of heavenly harmony and peace.

Nevertheless, there are two aspects of heaven which can never be properly glimpsed by those—whether poets or hermits—whose vision emerges only from solitary surrender to the beauty and tranquillity of the natural world. In the first place, heaven must surely be alive with people. It was Jean-Paul

Sartre whose play *Huis Clos* carried the message that "Hell is other people." Only in his or her most sinful moments can the Christian sympathize with that view. For the Christian, heaven must be other people. Hell must be the self, the confined, invulnerable, incommunicable, inescapable self. If love means anything at all, it involves relationship and community. The solitary dreamer, walking the hills alone, savoring alone the grandeur of the mountaintops, surveying the rolling and rising terrain beneath him, may find it a helpful therapy after a week in the busy factory or office. But to cultivate such experiences as a permanent route to happiness rather than a temporary relief from stress is to sell the soul.

Withdrawal from society can certainly be helpful and refreshing for men and women much occupied in activities with others, but lonely pleasures do not provide the right material for dreams of heaven. I believe C.S. Lewis says that coziness may be one of the delights of earthly life which heaven will simply not allow. Going private will not be a heavenly option. Indeed, perhaps the distinction between private and public is unknown in heaven. There no one can have anything to hide and the secrets of all hearts will be laid bare.

There is a second aspect of heaven which cannot be properly glimpsed in a vision conjured up from solitary surrender to the beauty of the natural world. Heaven is not the transfiguration of man the animal alone—the feeding, growing, breeding, dying creature of flesh and blood and bone. Heaven involves the transfiguration of man the maker. What man has made of his world by the exercise of his God-given brain and muscles is surely to be redeemed with him. What man has made which is worth making and has shown the divine spark of creativity in action will surely be preserved in some way. It is appropriate to picture man and woman in the Garden of Eden as naked creatures, totally unaccoutered against the background of flower and tree, bird and beast. But it would be absurd to picture heaven as a nature reserve.

Surely, the humanity which is to inhabit eternity when the

era of time is closed is a humanity with books and paintings, symphonies and cathedrals to its credit as well as lesser products of hand and mind. Though we have seen the absurdity of trying to picture ourselves carrying to heaven all the miscellany of earthly activity, it would be equally absurd to try to picture heaven as devoid of everything that distinguishes the life of civilized man from the life of the jungle. Heaven is no sunlit nudist colony.

The taming of nature through the development of agriculture and the building of civilized communities is as much a work inspired by the Holy Spirit as is the taming of man's inner appetites and lusts. The great work of molding and regulating natural forces to the service of man is wholly in tune with the work of molding and regulating human impulses to the service of God. Heaven must surely bring an awesomely wholesale judgment on the evils of our civilization. But it cannot demand the obliteration of civilization in favor of houseless, naked frolicking in a completely wild rural setting.

The Heavenly City

Surely this is what the apostle John recognized. He saw Babylon destroyed by the wrath of God. But, the city having been obliterated, there was no vision of healthy human life restored amid green meadows and bubbling brooks, shady trees and towering hills. The earthly city destroyed for its corruptions is superseded by the holy city. There can be no mistake about the source and authority of the holy city. It comes down from God himself.

The Bible opens in a garden and closes with the vision of a city. God gave humanity a paradise of natural beauty to dwell in. That was the beginning of the human story. When the experiment of creation is ended and the gates of the promised blessedness are opened to the redeemed, it is not a New Eden but a New Jerusalem that is prepared for them. There is no hint of a back-to-nature theme intruding into the Christian gospel.

There is no question of finally rolling back the record of civilization as a dismal blunder, no question of folding over the tale of history as a sad digression from divine purpose.

It is important to bear this in mind, because the apostle John's account of the destruction of Babylon is so horrendous. And it is fully in keeping with what the metropolis of all worldliness has become:

> Babylon the great is fallen, is fallen, and is become the habitation of devils, and the hold of every foul spirit, and a cage of every unclean and hateful bird. For all nations have drunk of the wine of the wrath of her fornication, and the kings of the earth have committed fornication with her, and the merchants of the earth are waxed rich through the abundance of her delicacies. (Rv 18:2-3)

The city is to be smitten with plagues, death, mourning, and famine. It will be consumed in fire, while the shipmasters who have been accustomed to trade by sea—carrying the rich cargoes that sustained its sumptuous lifestyle—shall stand far out off-shore in their vessels, marvelling and lamenting to see the smoke columning and ballooning into the air above the desolate ruins.

We do not need any great gifts of discernment to detect in the account of the destruction of Babylon a judgment to touch the nerve of twentieth-century mankind. We have our own colossal monuments to the sway of mammon over the kings of the earth. We have seen financiers and tycoons, media stars and politicians, professors and even bishops fornicating with the archwhore in whose embraces all ostensibly respectable endeavors are debauched into orgies of self-indulgence.

We have seen the smoke rising over defective nuclear installations and smelled death in the poisonous fumes escaping from leaks in chemical factories. Many of us daily partake in a life characterized by self-indulgent comfort and plenty which even the most affluent of the old Babylonian merchants might have envied. What would not one of them have paid for a flight across the world in a Concorde jet or a drive across a continent in a luxury car? We have enjoyed, and still enjoy, our daily meals in rooms to which the push of a button on our TV sets can bring graphic visual evidence of our fellow human beings suffering and dying by the thousands through famine and malnourishment.

We daily view the pornography of sex and violence disseminated in our supposedly civilized lands at newsstands and over the air waves. It penetrates into our homes and schools, soiling minds wherever it reaches. We are witnessing a consequent plague of sexual libertarianism that is eroding the health of the family, of the human mind, and now of the human body.

Babylon the Great *is* going to be destroyed. What nuclear war or nuclear accident might do to the fabric of our physical world, AIDS is doing to the fabric of the human body. When the smoke finally rises from this plague-stricken planet, will there be anyone out there in space to lament the fate of our desolate ruin?

It may not happen of course. For one thing, there is much good in our world as well as much evil. Indeed, there is much good in our civilization. But the Christian duties of faith and hope do not require us to close our minds to facts and our eyes to imminent dangers. If our metropolis of worldliness and corruption demands to be destroyed, no doubt it will be destroyed.

Christian faith and Christian hope are virtues which require us to cling to God when all else fails, when all else crumbles. Neither faith nor hope requires you to be convinced that our present civilization will not destroy itself. But both faith and hope require you to be convinced that even in the obliteration of our civilization, God's good purposes could yet be worked out. In any case, it ought never to be expected by Christians that if men and women by and large turn their backs on Christ's offer of redemption, the world can magically rescue itself from the destructive forces playing upon it. The ultimate goal of Christian hope is not a heaven on earth. The New

Jerusalem has a sure supernatural foundation.

Enmeshed as we are in a Babylonian civilization, should we not train ourselves to focus consciously on heaven's joys and wonders? Have we a duty to cultivate a yearning for heaven such as inspired Ann Griffiths? It goes against the grain. Most of us, I'm sure, feel a niggling doubt at the back of the mind when we sing hymns which paint heaven's peace as a welcome relief from earth's trials:

> Rest comes at length; though life be long and dreary,
>   The day must dawn, and darksome night be past;
> Faith's journey ends in welcome to the weary,
>   And heaven, our heart's true home, will come at last.

This is one of the popular hymns by the nineteenth century priest, Frederick W. Faber: "Hark, hark, my soul! Angelic songs are swelling." Its verses ring with the sound of angels' voices, calling out a welcome to us who are still "the pilgrims of the night." Do we feel like pilgrims of the night? Does life seem long and dreary? Does it not perhaps seem too short and too sweet? Since Faber himself died at the age of forty-nine, it seems sad to reflect that he had time to find life long and dreary.

I do not doubt Faber's fervent spirituality. It is reliably attested to in his work and in what is known of his life. There is another favorite hymn of his, "Souls of men, why will ye scatter?" which calls upon his fellow creatures to lay aside all the foolish reluctance and apprehension which cause them to run away from the Savior's love. The verses recapitulate testimony to God's mercy and kindness, to the forgiveness and joy God offers. They conclude:

> If our love were but more simple,
>   We should take him at his word;
> And our lives would be all sunshine
>   In the sweetness of our Lord.

Now it may be fair to claim that taking God at his word would flood our lives with sunshine, though in view of the physical and mental burdens some good souls have to bear, it seems a little simplistic to press the point so baldly. But I have myself sometimes felt the urge to examine the converse of this advice to take God at his word. Suppose God were to take me at my word! Am I sure that I really want him to? Suppose he chose the moment when I am singing in church:

Jerusalem, my happy home,
When shall I come to thee?
When shall my labours have an end,
Thy joys when shall I see?

Suppose that divine voice were suddenly to answer, calling out, "Tomorrow, at six o'clock in the morning precisely, if you really want to know!"

To be fair to the writer of this fine and very old hymn, his last verse shows that previous expressions of delight in the heavenly home have been rather a celebration of heaven's joy and wonder than a plea to be swiftly transported there:

O Christ, do thou my soul prepare
For that bright home of love
That I may see thee and adore,
With all thy saints above.

This must be accepted as a more heartfelt sentiment—this request to be duly prepared spiritually for the life hereafter— than eager requests for an early sight of the pearly gates and the streets of gold.

Whatever else heaven may be, it is certainly God's dwelling place. And our Christian duty is to yearn to be with God. It does not follow, however, that we must yearn to be in heaven here and now. For the Christian gospel essentially requires us to be linked to the living Christ. Two strands of thought,

156 / Knowing the Truth about Heaven and Hell

springing from two of our Lord's most forceful utterances, are relevant here. The first is that Christ is the vine of which we are the branches. Our lives are to be grafted into his.

The second is that, in leaving his disciples, Christ insisted that he would still be present with them. They were *not* instructed to abandon the world and the people around them. They were instructed to carry the gospel to the far corners of the world. No doubt the consummation of all Christian hopes and striving must lie in being received beyond time into the Savior's company and keeping. No doubt it is by faith and grace that such a consummation can be granted. But the servant who buried his single talent and came otherwise empty-handed to be greeted on his master's return got short shrift. It was the servant who had busied himself fruitfully during his master's absence and had turned five talents into ten whose fidelity was commended.

I would not wish to strain the detail of this parable in interpretation. Yet I cannot help reflecting that the servant who buried his talent did not neglect to ponder his future reunion with his master. Indeed he seems to have occupied his time mentally in making a false character study of his master and a false estimate of what the master would expect on his return.

In short, he planned his course of action so as to cut the right figure in his master's eyes. There was no failure to look forward. The mind of the enterprising servant must have been otherwise engaged. He was busily preoccupied with getting practical things done in his master's absence, and the consequence was that warmest of commendations: "Well done, thou good and faithful servant: ... enter thou into the joy of thy lord" (Mt 25:21).

With Christ in Glory

Entering into the joy of the Lord means being with Christ in glory. This is what Christians have always aspired to. We know that our lives ought to be one long experience of getting to know Christ and desiring to be with him and to know him in heaven. That is the logical culmination of all our efforts. Something needs to be said here in conclusion, therefore, about how best to focus on the Christ to whom we look for the fulfillment of all our hopes.

We look first to the Christ of the Gospels, the Christ made known to us in the pages of the New Testament. There is no need to try to list the words and acts of the Savior in order to show what it is that has drawn people to him throughout history as he drew them to himself during his years on earth. G.K. Chesterton said that what drew him to the study of Christ's life was the fact that everyone who spoke of him seemed to praise him for a different reason. What was the status of this man whom one person praised for his towering strength, another for his tender compassion, whom one person praised for his commanding authority, and another for his incredible humility?

Certainly the Christ made known to us week by week in public and private reading of the Scriptures, the Christ portrayed for us in a thousand sermons, should rightly call out in us a fervent longing to be more closely acquainted with him as teacher and healer, as friend and guide, as priest and suffering victim.

Yet, for all our efforts, the gap of two thousand years sets us at a distance from the Christ of the first century who walked the streets of Jerusalem and the dusty roads of Galilee. We have to reach out across the centuries in search of an intimate relationship with the Christ who sat in the house of Martha and Mary at Bethany, who paid a visit to Zacchaeus, and who distributed food to five thousand hungry people. Moreover, the awful mystery of the divine role on earth, of that progress from Bethlehem to Calvary for humanity's redemption, tends to exalt Christ almost above the grasp of familiar companionship. The demand for reverence is such that intimate personal affection can be all but submerged in awe.

But, of course, Christ is not just the Christ of the Sermon on the Mount and the agony in Gethsemane. He is the Christ with us today, distanced neither by centuries of history nor by a gap between earth and heaven. How readily we sense his presence and what kind of revelatory glimpses we get of him will depend on our own sensitivities to him. The poet Gerard Manley Hopkins looked out on the starry sky at night and saw the points of light as peepholes in the great wall of heaven, peepholes in the outer wall of the barn within which Christ is sitting at his harvest feast with his Spouse and his saints at the table. What a comfort to glimpse those glittering peepholes in the blackness of earth's night and to know what banquet the light is shining on.

We are not all poets gifted with imaginative insights like that. Nevertheless, Christ's presence is with all of us in the most accessible of forms—our own fellow men and women. It seems to me that without the constant reminder of this fact our attempt to stoke up an ardent longing to be with the Savior may fail under the strain of too lofty an effort. This is not to deny that some saints and mystics have found in solitude and in silent contemplation a relationship with Christ which may give them moments of ecstasy and which certainly floods their hearts with peace. For such Christians the desire to be with Christ in heaven is the longing to have these blissful contemplative experiences renewed and made permanent. But, just as we are not all poets for whom the stars are heaven's peepholes, so too we are not all contemplatives or religious who have tasted of the mystic's raptures.

We are all members of the body of Christ today, however. Through prayers, through worship, through the sacraments, we have our moments of which we can say "There Christ touched me! There Christ spoke to me! There I felt Christ's presence!" He requires that we seek him gradually through the discipline of worship, Bible study, prayer, and meditation. Then the presence of Christ can enter our lives, day by day building up a greater longing to know him more clearly and love him more dearly.

As Christ's body on earth, the members of his church are

called to show him forth in their day. If we have any doubts about our own ability to long to be with Christ in heaven, we should recall that everything worthwhile that every Christian has ever done for us was done by Christ. Did we have a Christian father who worked hard at great cost and self-sacrifice to give his children what was best for them? That was Christ shown forth in him. Did we have a Christian mother who loved us tenderly and nursed us devotedly through many an illness, perhaps one that might have cost our life? That was Christ shown forth in her. Did we have a teacher whose painstaking work illuminated the wonder of God's world for us and fired us with an earnest desire to learn? That was Christ shown forth in him or her. Did we have a priest, a pastor, or a minister who clearly and lovingly taught us the great truths of revelation and nurtured us in the Christian way? That was Christ shown forth in him.

Catherine of Siena, one of the great Christian mystics, wrote this to a newly ordained priest:

> Christ has no body now on earth but yours. No hands but yours. No feet but yours. Yours are the eyes through which his compassion must look out on the world. Yours are the feet with which he must go about doing good. Yours are the hands through which he must bless the world now.

It is not only God's chosen ministers who share this honor. It is all his faithful people. We have all encountered that body, clasped those hands, welcomed the approach of those feet, and been comforted by those eyes. For all the best that we have seen in our fellow Christians, all that we have genuinely loved in them, everything about their presence and their personality which we long to enjoy again—all that was the showing forth of Christ in them. The joy of heaven will be the renewing of all those relationships in the presence of him who was the source of everything that made them good and truly glorious.

The Christ we long for—the Christ whose touch has saved

us a thousand times from evil and from danger—is the Christ whose word made the path straight before us after our most desperate lapses into error or bewilderment. The Christ we long for is the Christ whose peace and reassurance descended upon us when our prayer was heard. The Christ we long for is the Christ whose light glowed in the eyes of all who have ever helped or comforted, cheered or loved us.

Do we long to be eternally in Christ's presence?

Is there anything else worth seeking?

Other Books in the
Knowing the Truth Series

Knowing the Truth of the Love of God
Peter Kreeft

God's love is the subject of Peter Kreeft's imaginative and thoughtful new book. With unusual clarity, he points out that the man or woman who begins to glimpse the God who is Redeemer, Creator, and Lover of our souls, will never be the same. He describes Scripture as a love story and then tells why divine love is the answer to our deepest problems.

Posing the hard questions about love that rankle the heart, Peter Kreeft never settles for easy answers. With eloquence and clarity of vision, he exposes today's superficial attitudes about love in order to lead people to a deeper understanding of what it means to be loved by God. *$7.95*

Knowing the Truth about the Resurrection
William L. Craig

Did Jesus rise from the dead? Is there proof for the resurrection? Are the accounts in the Gospels of Jesus' burial, the empty tomb, and his resurrection appearances reliable? Or are they biased? Can you explain away the resurrection appearances to the disciples as hallucinations? Or did the disciples really see Jesus?

William L. Craig candidly addresses these provocative questions and many more. Laying out the arguments, both pro and con, he presents a compelling case for the resurrection as an event of earth-shattering significance for the human race. If Jesus really rose and now lives, we can have a relationship with him that anticipates our own resurrection on the Last Day. Here is a convincing and compelling look at the resurrection for Christians and skeptics alike. *$7.95*